To.
Mrs K. Naresh
From
Sunita. Bhatia

Rodale's
BEST
RECIPES
1988

Rodale's BEST RECIPES 1988

by the
Editors of Rodale Press

Rodale Press, Emmaus, Pa.

Printed in the United States of America on recycled paper containing a high percentage of de-inked fiber.

Book Design by: Anita G. Patterson

Text Compiled by: Joan Bingham

Illustrations by: Jean Gardner

ISBN   0-87857-739-4   hardcover

2 4 6 8 10 9 7 5 3 1   hardcover

Contents

Introduction vi

Tempting and Unusual Breakfasts xviii
Down for the Count—Low-Calorie Recipes . . . 20
No-Meat Dishes 46
Fish and Fowl 68
Quick and Easy 100
Barbecues and Picnics 130
Beautiful Breads 156
Delicious Desserts 174

Index 196

Introduction

Every time someone reads a recipe in a Rodale publication, someone from the Rodale Food Center has read it first, tested it, tasted it, and sometimes, improved on it. Before these experts approve a recipe it must meet some very high standards. A dish may taste delicious, but unless it is nutritionally sound as well it will never be printed. Conversely, a recipe with a bevy of nutritional pluses is quickly discarded if it fails to pass the rigid flavor tests.

The Food Center is a busy, bustling place, headed by Tom Ney, a congenial graduate of the Culinary Institute of America. The superb cooks who work with him have a real willingness to try and try again in the search for perfection. During the year, these chefs test between 2,000 and 3,000 recipes.

Even excellent cooks sometimes write befuddling recipes because a step or procedure often seems so obvious to them that they won't mention it or explain it fully. So as the Food Center cooks prepare a dish they look for ways to clarify the recipe. For instance, they might specify the size of the pan or describe how brown the edges of a cake should be. They've discovered that there's an innate ambivalence in written recipes. In fact, two people using the same ingredients and making the same recipe often produce remarkably different foods.

The Food Center's professionals sometimes disagree about the degree of spiciness, sweetness, or other flavor judgments of a dish. But they don't rely on their opinions alone to determine the tastiness of a recipe. A panel of employees from different departments throughout the company does taste tests. This is one assignment for which there are plenty of volunteers!

Questions, We Get Questions

The folks at the Food Center answer numerous culinary questions annually that arise in producing Rodale magazines and books. Some questions are initiated by editors, while others come from readers. If our geniuses at the Food Center don't know an answer (which is rare), they seek out experts who do.

Here, with the answers, are some of the most interesting ones. As you can see, they cover quite a range and provide useful information on cooking and health not readily available elsewhere.

Question: Does adding a few pits to a jar of canned peaches really improve the fruit as I've heard it does?
Answer: Adding pits does change the flavor. Peaches canned with pits have a slight pungence, a little like almonds. Some people like it, others don't. However, we discourage this practice because someone might eat the kernels inside the pits. These kernels contain a substance called amygdalin, which can release cyanide.

Question: Can pesto be frozen successfully?
Answer: Yes. One of the best methods is to make a paste of just the basil leaves and a little oil, and freeze it in tablespoon-size dollops individually wrapped. That way, you can use the basil paste in recipes other than pesto. If you prefer, you can freeze the complete batch of pesto for a month or two. For long-term storage, omit garlic.

Question: Since I rarely eat red meat, only chicken and fish, as well as some grains, should I be taking amino-acid supplements?
Answer: All animal proteins are considered "complete." That means that the chicken and fish in your diet contain all of the nine essential amino acids your body needs.

Question: Does French bread with its crunchy crust have more fiber than other breads? What other breads have a lot of fiber?
Answer: Since most of the fiber in wheat flour is in the bran and germ, white-flour French bread doesn't offer much in added dietary fiber. Whole wheat flour has about five times as much fiber as white flour.

Question: Is there a way to keep fresh ginger root from molding in the refrigerator?

Answer: Ginger needs a temperature of 60°F to 65°F and 65 percent humidity. Unless you happen to have a spot that meets these needs, you're better off to freeze it. You can either slice it, wrap it, and freeze it, or wrap the whole root before freezing it. If you select the latter method, you can grate off little bits at a time.

Question: Is there any vitamin C left in a potato after it's baked?

Answer: Yes, although vitamin C is damaged by heat, in the specific conditions of baking a potato, 80 percent of the vitamin survives. A potato baked in the skin will provide about 29 percent of the U.S. RDA for vitamin C. The fresher the potato the better. After several months of storage, the vitamin C content drops sharply.

Question: Are untoasted almonds more nutritious than toasted almonds?

Answer: No. The differences are so small that they're insignificant. Untoasted almonds are ounce-for-ounce slightly higher in most B vitamins, but toasted almonds are slightly higher in folate, iron, zinc, copper, vitamin E, and fiber.

Question: Is tomato sauce or paste a good source of vitamin C even after it's cooked again?

Answer: Yes, because tomatoes are a very good source of vitamin C to begin with, and because tomato sauce and paste are fairly concentrated. To maximize the vitamin C in your tomato sauce, don't cook it more than necessary, use stainless-steel cookware, and keep the sauce covered.

Question: I've heard that you lose most of the nutritional benefits of vegetables after you peel them. Is that true of carrots? You can see the orange-colored carotene and it certainly goes deeper than the peel.

Answer: Peeling a carrot removes about 10 percent of its weight and therefore roughly 10 percent of its carotene. There's no special concentration near the surface.

(continued)

Questions, We Get Questions—Continued

Question: What does microwave cooking do to vitamins?
Answer: In cooking vegetables it depends on the amount of water you use. If you use less water than you do for conventional cooking, you'll have less nutritional loss. For cooking meat there's no tidy rule. Vitamin retention may be high or low depending on the meat and the vitamin.

Question: Should I throw away potatoes with green spots or can I just cut away the green?
Answer: If half or more of the potato is green, throw the whole thing away. If the green patches are smaller, you can cut them out as long as you remove a thick slice of the flesh underneath each green part. The green is chlorophyll and is in itself harmless, but it heralds the presence of two bitter-tasting toxins, solanine and chaconine. In large amounts these make some people very sick. Neither baking nor boiling will destroy the toxins.

Question: What's the best way to store mushrooms? Can I freeze them?
Answer: Store fresh whole mushrooms in a brown paper bag in the refrigerator. Don't use a plastic bag because it creates a moisture chamber ideal for growing microbes that make mushrooms spoil. Yes, you can freeze mushrooms. Wash and slice them and place them in a freezer bag. Press out the air and seal. If you plan to store them for longer than three months, pour diluted lemon juice over the slices and blanch them for 2½ minutes in boiling water before you wrap them. Cook mushrooms unthawed.

Question: Can I substitute short- and long-grain rice one for the other?
Answer: The two types have different cooking characteristics, mainly because they have different ratios of starches. Long-grain rice remains in separate grains because of its amylose starch. Medium- and short-grain rice are stickier because they contain amylopectin. Other than for frying, when you should use short-grain rice, you can usually substitute one for the other, but the texture will be different.

Question: I really enjoy East Indian food and have been trying to learn how to cook it. I notice that many recipes call for ghee instead of butter. Does it contain less cholesterol?

Answer: Tablespoon for tablespoon, ghee actually contains a little more cholesterol than butter. Ghee is the Indian version of clarified butter. To make it, the milk solids and moisture are separated from the butter during long, slow heating, leaving pure butterfat.

Question: How can I remove garlic odor from my wooden cutting board?

Answer: There are four frequently recommended methods: One is to wash the board with a mixture of equal parts of bleach and water. Leave solution on for a minute or two and rinse well with water. The second method is to rub the board with a paste made with equal parts borax and salt, then rinse well with clear water. Other cooks prefer to use a paste of baking soda and water. And, finally, pure lemon juice is the choice of some people.

Question: How can I store Jerusalem artichokes? Do they freeze well?

Answer: Freezing isn't the answer. The chokes will lose their famous crunch. The best way is to wash the chokes, drying them thoroughly. You can even use a hair dryer for this. Then put the tubers in a plastic bag with several holes punched in it, and store the chokes in the vegetable drawer of the refrigerator. They should keep from 10 days to a month.

Question: Is there really caffeine in chocolate? I've never seen it listed in the ingredients.

Answer: Chocolate does contain caffeine, but it's a natural component of the cocoa bean, so the caffeine doesn't have to be listed among the ingredients. The amount of caffeine in chocolate is quite small, however, and other compounds such as fats have more dietary impact than the caffeine.

Maximizing Flavor

We don't use salt in any of our recipes because there's just too much evidence that it is a factor in high blood pressure for certain people. Our recipes are seasoned with healthful herbs and spices.

Like the people at the Rodale Food Center, you no doubt have a favorite herb. One of the staff loves basil and adds a touch of it whenever possible. Another chef prefers dill, while still another opts for tarragon. But don't get hung up on one herb to the exclusion of the others. They offer such wonderful variety.

A well-stocked herb and spice rack sounds like a good idea. But remember, these condiments are fragile. They don't respond well to either heat or light, so buy them in small quantities and keep them in a dry, dark place. It's a good idea to replace herbs and spices every three months or so to get the maximum flavor from them. Sometimes outdated spices or herbs can ruin the taste of the finished dish.

One favorite flavoring trick in the Rodale Food Center that you might like to try is to keep a peppermill filled with mustard seed and keep a sprinkling of other spice seeds on the range to give a quick kick to foods while they're cooking.

Microwave Magic

Over the past few years, the microwave appliance has become a standard feature in many households. The Food Center offers these simple tips on using it as a time-saver.

❖ Whenever you cook more than one kind of vegetable at a time, cut all the vegetable pieces the same size. Combining vegetables with similar textures helps, too. Then you can cook all of them together and they'll be done at the same time.

❖ To peel fresh tomatoes (a pesky job), microwave them on full power for about 1 minute and the peel will slip off easily. The time may need to be adjusted slightly depending upon the size and ripeness of the tomato.

❖ For a fast, nutritious, low-calorie dessert, bake an apple. Peel the top third to prevent the inside from bursting through the skin as the heat expands it. Cover the apple and cook it on full power for 3 minutes. Serve with yogurt, flavored with maple syrup and cinnamon.

❖ Dried fruits are packed with vitamins and minerals. To plump raisins and other dried fruits, lightly sprinkle one cup of dried fruit with fruit juice or water. Cover it lightly and microwave on full power for 1 minute, stirring after about 30 seconds. Let the fruit stand about 4 minutes before using it in baking, on cereals, in compotes, or as a snack.

❖ Nuts are a fine concentrated source of protein, vitamins, and minerals. But shelling them is a nuisance. To shell nuts easily, place a handful in a dish with enough water to cover them. Cover the dish lightly, and microwave on full power for 4 to 5 mintues. Drain, let nuts cool and dry, then shell them. Shell chestnuts by slitting the shells, then microwaving a handful, uncovered, on high for about 45 seconds.

❖ If you want to prevent the possibility of failure in a bread recipe by checking to see if the yeast is alive, mix it with the sweetener, liquid, and ¼ cup of the recipe's flour. Microwave on lowest power, lightly covered, for 1 minute. If alive, it will bubble up just as it does with the conventional method.

❖ To preserve nutrients in sauces, cut down on the cooking time. Microwaved sauces cook faster in a measuring cup than in a shallow dish.

All Fats Aren't Created Equal

These days, people are watching fat more than they are calories, and the subject has become a confusing one. The fact is that all fats aren't equally bad for you, and some fat is necessary in your diet. Saturated fats, most often found in protein-rich foods of animal origins, such as red meats, full-fat dairy products, and eggs, are considered the worst.

Polyunsaturated fats found in other vegetables and animal foods seem to have a modest cholesterol-lowering effect—so it's wise to switch from saturated fats to polyunsaturated fats wherever possible.

The good news is that recent studies suggest that olive oil, a monounsaturated fat, once thought to be more or less neutral, may actually lower cholesterol more effectively than polyunsaturated fats.

The Cook's Guide to Oils

Oil	Flavor	Suggested Uses	Comments	Approximate Smoking Point
Almond	mildly sweet and nutty; very light, if refined	dressing for greens, vegetables; not good for cooking	contains about 70% monounsaturated fats; one of the lowest in saturated fats (8%)	
Avocado	sweet walnut-like flavor	vinaigrette salad dressing, or mix with fresh lemon juice for bitter greens, such a arugula, chicory, watercress; not good for cooking	keeps a strong flavor even when refined; 62% monounsaturated fats	
Corn	light, bland	deep and shallow frying; mix with strong-flavored oils in dressing; popping corn; basting	most versatile oil for all-purpose uses; 59% unsaturated fats	465°F

Selecting Cooking Oils

The oils you cook in, use for flavoring, or to dress salads can completely change the character of the dish in which you're using them. We've rated some of the more popular ones so you'll know how to use them.

Now for the wonderful recipes from our Rodale Food Center. Enjoy!

Oil	Flavor	Suggested Uses	Comments	Approximate Smoking Point
Hazelnut	buttery	dressings for salads, raw vegetables	very high in monounsaturated fats (78%)	
Olive	light to fruity to peppery (green olive oil)	frying breaded vegetables; pasta sauces, salad dressings, mayonnaise; sprinkled over Italian soups, baked chicken, or baked-fish casseroles	if you buy gallon tins, decant olive oil into smaller dark-glass bottles; 74% monounsaturated fats	375°F
Peanut	distinctly nutty	deep and shallow frying; dressings for raw vegetables; in potato salads	46% monounsaturated fats; 32% polyunsaturated fats	440°F

(continued)

The Cook's Guide to Oils—Continued

Oil	Flavor	Suggested Uses	Comments	Approximate Smoking Point
Safflower	bland	deep and shallow frying; greasing baking tins; popping corn; to cut strong-flavored oils in cold dressings	very rich in linoleic acid (usually 70%); a polyunsaturated fat	510°F
Sesame seed	toasty, earthy, robust flavor	as a seasoning for cooked dishes, especially Chinese stir-fry; in marinades; along with other mild oil in salad dressing; not good for frying	only the "burnt-toast"-colored Oriental sesame oil has the unmistakable distinct flavor; clear, refined sesame is very light tasting; 42% polyunsaturated fats	420°F
Soy	sweet beany flavor	deep and shallow frying; greasing tins; popping corn	the dark cold-pressed soy oil is much beanier and tends to foam when used in frying (it also contains more lecithin); 58% polyunsaturated fats	495°F

Oil	Flavor	Suggested Uses	Comments	Approximate Smoking Point
Sunflower	mild hint of raw sunflower seeds	baked goods, shallow frying, mild salad dressings	percentage of polyunsaturated fats may range from 40% to 65%	480°F
Walnut	butternut flavor	dressings with fruit-flavored vinegars for mixed greens, raw or steamed vegetables; not good for cooking	imported has a strong flavor, clear refined is more bland; 63% polyunsaturated fats	

Tempting and Unusual Breakfasts

Breakfast is touted as the most important meal of the day. Yet many people skip it because: they find breakfast food boring; they don't think they can afford the time for breakfast; or they think it will help with weight control. The recipes that follow will make even the most jaded breakfast-skipper reconsider. And some of the recipes are super-fast!

But why is breakfast so important? What's wrong with gulping down a cup of coffee and a glass of juice or just missing breakfast altogether?

In addition to improving your mental acuity, breakfast makes a significant contribution to your daily nutrient intake, one that isn't made up easily at lunch or dinner.

Dieters who make the mistake of doing without breakfast are usually so hungry by lunchtime that they eat more than they would have for breakfast and lunch combined. But in addition to that, the body burns breakfast rations more efficiently than the calories it consumes at other meals. Another reason why avoiding breakfast is a poor strategy for losing weight: if you go for long stretches without eating, your body responds by slowing its metabolism and actually burns calories more slowly.

Fast-Fix Blender Breakfasts

If your morning routine is truly so rushed that you just don't have the time to cook any breakfast, your blender can bail you out. It provides a world of fast, easy, and delicious breakfasts at the touch of a switch. All of the ones in this chapter offer enough protein, carbohydrates, vitamins, and minerals to keep you feeling satisfied and energetic right up until lunchtime.

You can use the chart to come up with easy blends. Simply toss the ingredients into the blender and process for about 20 seconds or until the mix looks smooth. You can use both milk and yogurt as shown in the chart, substitute cottage cheese for the yogurt, or double the amount of either one and skip the other. Use low-fat or skim-milk products to keep a lid on calories. The amounts given in the chart make one serving, but you can double or triple the amounts to serve more people or to make enough extra for a quick start on another morning.

Crepes, Pancakes, and Waffles

While pancakes and waffles are old standards, crepes have become popular in the last few years. And we love them! The toppings and fillings you can use to vary them are only limited by your imagination.

Despite their French name and gourmet mystique, crepes are really just thin pancakes. They're so adaptable, they can be served at almost any meal. But breakfast gets our vote. Begin with a properly made crepe (page 16), then add whichever fillings or toppings suit your fancy.

Easy Crepes Creations

Fillings

❖ Cooked fish, shellfish, or poultry
❖ Cooked vegetables
❖ Scrambled eggs with dill
❖ Stewed dried fruits
❖ Chopped fresh fruits
❖ Shredded cheeses
❖ Ricotta cheese
❖ Apple-prune butter
❖ Applesauce

Toppings

❖ Yogurt
❖ Tomato sauce
❖ Maple whipped cream
❖ Cooked fish or poultry, creamed
❖ Strawberry or raspberry sauce
❖ Honey-apple topping
❖ Sauteed mushrooms
❖ Chopped fresh fruit
❖ Lemon or orange peel, finely grated

Fast-Fix Blender Breakfasts

Milk	Yogurt	Fruit	Sweetener	Extra
½ cup	½ cup	½ apple, chopped	1 teaspoon maple syrup	dash of cinnamon
½ cup	½ cup	¼ cup chopped apricots	1 teaspoon maple syrup	dash of nutmeg
½ cup	½ cup	½ cup chopped peaches	1 teaspoon maple syrup	dash of nutmeg
½ cup	½ cup	1 medium-size banana	1 teaspoon honey	dash of grated orange peel
½ cup	½ cup	½ cup chopped papaya	1 teaspoon honey	dash of grated orange peel
½ cup	½ cup	½ cup chopped honeydew melon	1 teaspoon honey	dash of lime juice
½ cup	½ cup	½ cup chopped cantaloupe	1 teaspoon honey	dash of lemon juice
½ cup	½ cup	½ cup chopped pineapple	1 teaspoon honey	dash of lemon juice
½ cup	½ cup	½ cup chopped pears	1 teaspoon honey	1 drop mint extract
½ cup	½ cup	¼ cup chopped avocado	1 teaspoon honey	½ teaspoon lemon juice
¼ cup	¼ cup	½ cup prune juice	1 teaspoon honey	dash of grated lemon peel
¼ cup	¼ cup	½ cup orange juice	1 teaspoon maple syrup	1 drop vanilla extract

Pancakes and waffles are made easily from a batter spooned onto a hot, oiled griddle. Pancakes are usually lightened with baking powder, baking soda, or beaten egg whites, though sometimes they're made with yeast.

Before you pour the batter for waffles or pancakes, make sure the griddle or waffle iron is hot enough to make drops of cold water dance when they're dropped onto the surface.

Flip pancakes when the bubbles that form on the tops have burst and the bottoms are light brown.

Waffles should be cooked without opening the iron until it has stopped steaming.

We're pleased that the recipes in this chapter provide something for the adventurous eater as well as for the more conventional among us.

Banana Whiz

2 SERVINGS

1 cup plain low-fat yogurt	1 banana, sliced
½ cup orange juice	1 tablespoon honey
½ cup skim milk	dash of ground cinnamon

Process all ingredients in a food processor or blender until smooth.

Breakfast Cappuccino

2 SERVINGS

1 cup skim milk	½ teaspoon ground cinnamon
2 teaspoons instant decaffeinated coffee	½ teaspoon vanilla extract
2 tablespoons honey	4 ice cubes

Process all ingredients in a food processor or blender until smooth.

Carob Eggnog

2 SERVINGS

1½ cups plain low-fat yogurt	½ teaspoon vanilla extract
1 tablespoon carob powder	1 egg
2 tablespoons honey	dash of ground nutmeg

Process all ingredients in a food processor or blender until smooth.

Peanut Butter Shake

2 SERVINGS

1 cup low-fat cottage cheese
1 cup milk
⅓ cup peanut butter

1 tablespoon honey
1 teaspoon vanilla extract

Process all ingredients in a food processor or blender until smooth.

Raspberry Delight

2 SERVINGS

2 cups plain low-fat yogurt
1 cup fresh or frozen raspberries
(tightly packed)

1 tablespoon honey
½ teaspoon vanilla extract

Process all ingredients in a food processor or blender until smooth.

"Rubyburst" Juice

2 TO 3 SERVINGS

1 cup cranberry-apple juice
1 cup cranberry-raspberry juice
¼ cup orange juice

2 strips orange peel
2 whole cloves
1 stick of cinnamon

In a small saucepan, combine juices, orange peel, cloves, and cinnamon. Bring to a boil over medium heat, then reduce heat and simmer for 20 minutes. Strain into warm mugs and serve immediately.

Apples and Oats

4 SERVINGS

enough oat bran cereal and
water to make 4 servings
½ cup currants
1 apple, grated

1 tablespoon maple syrup
½ teaspoon ground caraway seeds,
optional
½ teaspoon ground cinnamon

Begin to cook oat bran and water according to package directions. When you take it off the heat to let it stand, add currants, apples, maple syrup, caraway, and cinnamon. Stir to combine. Let stand as directed, then serve immediately.

Banana Splits with Apricot Cream

4 SERVINGS

The apricot cream can be made ahead. It will keep well in the refrigerator for about five days.

Apricot Cream
16 ounces low-fat cottage cheese
3 tablespoons apricot jam

Banana Splits
4 bananas
1 cup fresh strawberries
1 cup fresh blueberries
toasted wheat germ or sliced toasted almonds, to sprinkle

To prepare the apricot cream: Scoop cottage cheese into a food processor or blender and process until smooth. This may take a couple of minutes. Add jam and process again. Refrigerate overnight to allow flavors to mingle.

To prepare the banana splits: At breakfast time, just before serving, split bananas lengthwise, setting each pair on a separate plate. Scoop some apricot cream on each split banana. Slice strawberries and add them, along with the blueberries, to splits. Top with wheat germ or almonds and serve.

Breakfast Fruit Kabobs

4 SERVINGS

You can take your choice of fruit for this delicious breakfast treat. Try melon balls, citrus sections, or whole strawberries combined with pear chunks, apples, or bananas.

3¾ cups mixed fresh fruit chunks
1 lime, thinly sliced
½ cup plain low-fat yogurt
2 teaspoons lime juice

1 teaspoon honey
¼ teaspoon freshly grated nutmeg
mint sprigs for garnish

In a large bowl, toss fruit with the lime slices. Then thread attractively on 6-inch skewers.

In a small bowl, combine yogurt, lime juice, honey, and nutmeg. Either drizzle sauce over fruit or serve it in a bowl. Garnish with mint.

Broccoli and Potato Frittata

4 SERVINGS

2 teaspoons butter or margarine
1 cup diced cooked potatoes
10 ounces frozen chopped broccoli, thawed
¼ cup chopped scallions
1 clove garlic, minced
6 eggs or 1½ cups egg substitute

3 tablespoons water
1 tablespoon minced fresh parsley
2 tablespoons shredded cheddar or grated Parmesan cheese

Melt butter or margarine in a large ovenproof skillet. Add potatoes, broccoli, scallions, and garlic. Cover and cook for 7 to 10 minutes, stirring occasionally.

In a small bowl, beat eggs with water and parsley. Pour into skillet and cook over low heat until bottom is set and lightly browned (run a spatula around the edge of eggs to let uncooked portion run underneath).

Place skillet under broiler until eggs are golden on top. Sprinkle with cheese and broil until melted.

Barley Pilaf with Grilled Apples

6 SERVINGS

This pilaf can be made the night before and reheated, moistened with a little juice, when you're ready for breakfast.

Pilaf
1 teaspoon unsalted butter
1 cup barley
⅛ teaspoon ground cinnamon
   dash of freshly ground nutmeg
   seeds of 1 cardamom pod,
     crushed
1 vanilla bean
1½ cups apple juice
1½ cups water

Apples
2 baking apples
   apple juice
   ground cinnamon for
     sprinkling

To prepare the pilaf: Melt butter in a medium-size saucepan. Add barley, cinnamon, nutmeg, cardamom, and vanilla and saute until fragrant, about 2 minutes. Add apple juice and water and bring pilaf to a boil. Reduce heat, cover saucepan, and let simmer for 45 to 60 minutes. (The time will depend on the type of saucepan you're using, the type of barley you've selected, and the source of heat.) Take a peek into the pot after 45 minutes to see if all the liquid has been absorbed. If not, continue cooking and checking.

To prepare the apples: Core and cut apples into thin, round slices. Sprinkle with apple juice and cinnamon and broil for about 3 minutes. Flip them over, sprinkle again, and grill for about 2 minutes more. Serve apples hot with pilaf.

VARIATION: Use peach slices instead of apples and grill for only half the time.

Eggs with Chili Sauce

4 SERVINGS

These scrambled eggs served with cooked chilies make a colorful and spicy breakfast dish. Serve them with tortillas or pita, and provide avocado slices, chopped scallions, and grated cheese as accompaniments.

1 onion, minced	¼ cup chopped fresh coriander
1 clove garlic, minced	½ teaspoon dried oregano
1 teaspoon olive oil	6 eggs, slightly beaten, or 1½
12 romaine lettuce leaves,	cups egg substitute
coarsely chopped	1 cup plain low-fat yogurt
3 red or green chilies, chopped	

In a large nonstick skillet, cook onions and garlic in oil until limp. Add romaine, chilies, coriander, and oregano. Cook for about 3 minutes, or until lettuce has wilted. Remove from heat.

Coat a nonstick skillet with vegetable cooking spray. Add eggs and stir over low heat until lightly scrambled.

Place the eggs in center of a large serving platter and arrange chili mixture around them. Serve topped with yogurt.

Corn Pone Pie

6 TO 12 SERVINGS

Serve this Southern specialty warm with Tomato Chutney (recipe follows).

1½ cups yellow cornmeal	2 tablespoons minced fresh
1 cup unbleached white flour	parsley
1 tablespoon baking powder	1½ cups buttermilk
½ teaspoon turmeric	¼ cup honey
3 allspice berries, ground	2 tablespoons vegetable oil
½ cup cooked corn kernels	1 egg or ¼ cup egg substitute
¼ cup minced scallions	

In a medium-size bowl, sift together cornmeal, flour, baking powder, turmeric, and allspice. Add corn, scallions, and parsley, mixing well until combined.

In a small bowl, mix together buttermilk, honey, oil, and egg. Pour into dry ingredients. Using a large rubber spatula, work quickly to combine the mixtures.

Coat a 9-inch pie plate with vegetable cooking spray. Transfer batter to pie plate. Level top by tapping batter with your fingertips (a true pone technique). Bake at 375°F for about 25 minutes, or until a knife inserted into the center comes out clean.

Tomato Chutney

3 CUPS

5 tomatoes (about 2 pounds), peeled and chopped
½ cup minced red onions
½ cup chopped celery
1 bay leaf
1 tablespoon apple juice

2 tart green apples, coarsely chopped
¼ cup apple cider vinegar
½ teaspoon ground cinnamon
4 allspice berries, crushed

In a medium-size saucepan, combine tomatoes, onions, celery, bay leaf, and apple juice. Simmer 5 minutes. Add apples, vinegar, cinnamon, and allspice. Partially cover and simmer 40 minutes, stirring frequently.

Pastacake

4 SERVINGS

This is called Two Sides Brown in China, where it is enjoyed as breakfast and as a snack. It's great use for spaghetti from the night before.

5 medium-size dried apricots, chopped (about ¼ cup)
2 tablespoons golden raisins, chopped

dash of sesame oil
3 cups cooked spaghetti
1 egg, beaten
1 tablespoon apple juice

In a large bowl, combine all ingredients. Using your hands, work the mixture so that it's moist all over and the fruit is distributed throughout.

Spray a 10-inch nonstick skillet with vegetable cooking spray and add pasta mixture. Pat it down into a pancake, set a 10-inch plate on it, weight the plate with a heavy object, and cook over medium heat for about 10 minutes.

To flip the pastacake, which is easier than you may think, first remove the heavy object. Then pick up the skillet in one hand, hold the plate securely with the other, and reverse positions so the plate is on the bottom and the skillet is (upside down) on top.

Put the skillet back on the burner and, with the plate right next to it, slide the pastacake right in. Set the plate and the weight on top and cook for 10 minutes more, taking care not to burn the fruit. When the pastacake is ready, slide it onto a plate and cut into wedges with kitchen shears.

VARIATIONS: Use chopped fresh or dried apples or pears instead of apricots.

Herb-Pressed Corn Cakes

6 SERVINGS

Cakes
½ cup cornmeal
½ cup unbleached white flour
1 cup buttermilk
8 herb sprigs (thyme, dill,
      marjoram, parsley, or chives)

Sauce
½ cup plain low-fat yogurt
1 teaspoon tomato paste
1 tablespoon minced fresh chives

To prepare the cakes: In a medium-size bowl, combine cornmeal, flour, and buttermilk. Spray a nonstick skillet with vegetable cooking spray and heat over medium-high heat. Drop in about ¼ cup batter for each cake (you may need to do this in 2 batches), gently press an herb sprig into the top of each one, and cook until golden and slightly crisp. Then flip cakes and cook for several minutes more.

To prepare the sauce: Combine yogurt, tomato paste, and chives.

Serve cakes immediately, accompanied by sauce.

VARIATIONS: Use slivers of yellow and red tomato, green pepper, or kernels of cooked corn instead of herbs.

Raspberry Bread Pudding

6 SERVINGS

4 slices whole wheat bread	2 eggs
⅓ cup toasted wheat germ	2 tablespoons maple syrup
2 tablespoons bran	1 teaspoon vanilla extract
2 cups fresh raspberries	plain low-fat yogurt for topping,
1 cup orange juice	optional
1 cup skim milk	

Preheat oven to 375°F.

Spray a 1½-quart baking dish with vegetable cooking spray. Tear bread into 1-inch pieces and place in prepared dish along with wheat germ, bran, and raspberries. Toss to mix.

In a medium-size bowl, whisk together orange juice, milk, eggs, maple syrup, and vanilla. Pour over bread mixture, pressing bread into liquid. Bake 40 to 45 minutes, or until all liquid has been absorbed. Serve warm topped with yogurt.

Prune Butter

2 CUPS

This is a wonderful topping for muffins, scones, pancakes, or waffles, and it is a delicious dip for apple or pear slices.

2 cups pitted prunes	pinch of freshly grated orange
1¾ cups apple juice	peel
4 dried figs, stems removed	extra apple juice for thinning,
1 vanilla bean	if necessary

In a medium-size saucepan, combine prunes, 1¾ cups apple juice, figs, vanilla bean, and orange peel. Bring mixture to a gentle simmer and cook over low heat, stirring frequently, for 30 minutes.

Let mixture cool slightly. Remove and discard vanilla bean, then scoop mixture into a food processor or blender. Puree until smooth and butterlike, adding more apple juice if it becomes too thick.

Prune Compote

2 TO 4 SERVINGS

Serve this as a side dish, or use it to top French toast or waffles.

1 cup pitted jumbo prunes
½ cup apple juice

4 teaspoons lime juice
1 1-inch piece cinnamon stick

Combine prunes, apple juice, lime juice, and cinnamon in a small saucepan. Simmer for 5 to 7 minutes, or until prunes have plumped slightly and sauce has thickened a bit. Remove cinnamon stick before serving.

Raisin and Sweet Potato Scones

1½ DOZEN SCONES

½ cup whole wheat flour
½ cup unbleached white flour
¼ cup corn bran
½ teaspoon baking soda
1 teaspoon cream of tartar
    pinch of ground cinnamon
    pinch of ground nutmeg

½ cup chopped raisins
½ cup grated peeled sweet
    potatoes
2 tablespoons safflower oil
⅓ cup plus 1 tablespoon
    buttermilk

Preheat oven to 475°F.
In a large mixing bowl, combine whole wheat flour, unbleached white flour, corn bran, baking soda, cream of tartar, cinnamon, nutmeg, raisins, and sweet potatoes. Stir in oil and buttermilk until blended. With floured hands, knead mixture for 2 minutes.
On a lightly floured surface, roll out dough to a generous ¼-inch thickness. Cut out 2½-inch rounds, setting each round on a lightly oiled baking sheet as you go. Use all the dough by rerolling scraps. Bake scones for 6 to 8 minutes. Serve with Prune Butter (page 14).

Whole Wheat Crepes

12 CREPES

These can be made ahead and either refrigerated or frozen until you want to use them. To store, place a piece of waxed paper between each crepe, then wrap stack in plastic wrap. Heat for a few seconds in a microwave before serving.

1½ cups skim milk
2 eggs

½ teaspoon ground cinnamon
1 cup whole wheat pastry flour

Place milk, eggs, cinnamon, and flour in a blender. Process on medium speed until smooth, stopping and scraping down sides with a spatula as necessary. Refrigerate container for 30 minutes.

Process again briefly. Pour about 2 or 3 tablespoons of batter into a heated, lightly oiled crepe pan. Swirl pan gently to spread a thin layer of batter across the bottom. Cook crepe for about 1 minute over medium heat, or until the surface appears dry and the bottom is golden brown. Invert the pan over a cake rack covered with a kitchen towel. Repeat with remaining batter, blending the batter briefly before making each crepe.

Fruity Crepes

6 SERVINGS

2½ cups low-fat cottage cheese
2 tablespoons maple syrup
½ teaspoon finely grated lemon peel
¼ teaspoon vanilla extract
12 Whole Wheat Crepes (above)

2 cups sliced fresh strawberries
1 cup fresh blueberries
½ cup halved seedless grapes
mint sprigs for garnish

In a medium-size bowl, beat together cottage cheese, maple syrup, lemon peel, and vanilla. Place about 3 tablespoons of filling on edge of each crepe and roll up.

Combine strawberries, blueberries, and grapes in a medium-size bowl. Arrange crepes seam side down on a large serving platter. Spoon fruit over crepes. Garnish with mint.

Steamed Breakfast Wontons

6 SERVINGS

This is an easy introduction to *Dim Sum,* which is traditionally early-day teahouse food. To save time in the morning, prepare the filling the evening before.

Wontons
9 ounces boneless, skinless
   chicken breasts
¼ cup minced scallions
1 teaspoon low-sodium soy
   sauce
¼ teaspoon honey
¼ teaspoon grated ginger root
1 clove garlic, minced
2 slices ginger root
1 scallion, coarsely chopped
24 round wonton skins

Sauce
3 tablespoons low-sodium soy
   sauce
3 tablespoons water
½ teaspoon sesame oil, optional

To prepare the wontons: In a food processor, combine chicken, minced scallions, soy sauce, honey, grated ginger, and garlic until pureed.

Place ginger slices and chopped scallions in a wide, deep saucepan. Add about an inch of water. Place a steamer rack in the pan. Cover and bring water to a boil while you assemble wontons.

Place 1 teaspoon of filling in the center of each wonton skin. Lightly moisten circumference with water so edges stick together. Pleat edges of wonton around filling, so wonton resembles an impressionistic flower. Steam wontons in batches, covered, for 8 to 10 minutes.

To prepare the sauce: In a small bowl, combine soy sauce, water, and oil if desired. Partially dip warm wontons in sauce.

Rice Waffles with Strawberry Sauce

4 TO 6 SERVINGS

Stack these fiber-rich waffles to form a "cake," and serve with hot mint tea.

Strawberry Sauce
1   12-ounce package
      unsweetened frozen
      strawberries
2   teaspoons cornstarch
½   teaspoon lemon juice
1   tablespoon honey, or to taste

Waffles
2   cups whole wheat flour
2   teaspoons baking powder
½   teaspoon baking soda
1   egg or ¼ cup egg substitute
1⅔ cups buttermilk
2   tablespoons vegetable oil
1   cup cooked brown rice

Assembly
1¼ cups low-fat cottage cheese

To prepare the sauce: Thaw the berries, reserving the liquid. Mix 1 tablespoon of the liquid with the cornstarch in a small saucepan. Add remaining liquid, lemon juice, and berries. Bring to a boil, stirring constantly, and cook until thick. Stir in honey. Set aside.

To prepare the waffles: In a medium-size bowl, stir together flour, baking powder, and baking soda.

In another bowl, beat together egg, buttermilk, and oil until smooth. Pour into flour mixture and mix well. Stir in the rice. Bake in a preheated waffle iron (following manufacturer's instructions). Set aside baked waffles, keeping them warm.

To assemble: Press the cottage cheese through a fine sieve to break up curds.

Place 1 large waffle (do not separate individual waffles) on a serving plate. Spread on a layer of cottage cheese. Top with another waffle. Spread on a layer of strawberry mixture. Continue stacking, ending with strawberry mixture. Top with a dollop of cottage cheese. Slice into wedges to serve.

Cinnamon Caraway Pancakes

4 TO 6 SERVINGS

Pancakes
½ cup whole wheat flour
½ cup unbleached white flour
1 teaspoon baking powder
½ teaspoon ground caraway seeds
½ teaspoon ground cinnamon
⅓ cup golden raisins
1 medium-size apple, minced
1 egg or ¼ cup egg substitute
½ cup buttermilk
½ cup plain low-fat yogurt
2 tablespoons maple syrup

Sauce
¼ cup plain low-fat yogurt
1 teaspoon maple syrup

To prepare the pancakes: In a medium-size bowl, sift together whole wheat flour, unbleached white flour, baking powder, caraway, and cinnamon. Add raisins and apples, mixing well.

In a small bowl, combine egg, buttermilk, yogurt, and maple syrup. Add to dry ingredients. Using a large rubber spatula, work quickly to combine mixtures.

Lightly oil a large nonstick skillet and heat over medium-high heat. Drop tablespoonfuls of batter into skillet. Cook 2 to 3 minutes, then flip pancakes and continue cooking until browned and puffed.

To prepare the sauce: In a small bowl, mix together yogurt and maple syrup.

Arrange pancakes on heated platter and drizzle with sauce. Serve immediately.

Down
for the Count–
Low-Calorie
Recipes

The emphasis on light foods is increasing, and here we have a group of recipes that embraces light, low-fat meals and eschews fad diets. They prove that well-planned recipes can be low in calories yet elegant and tasty when light ingredients are substituted for heavy ones.

Many people believe that adding fat to food is the best way to add flavor. They sauté everything in butter and oils and add heavy cheeses to salads and creams to soups, stews, and casseroles. (No wonder 40 percent of the calories in the average American diet comes from fat. And a good bit of that 40 percent is added during cooking.) That's yesterday's thinking. Today we know there are numerous ways to cut back on fat in cooking.

Incorporate the following tips and make them part of your everyday eating style, and you'll be cutting back on fat but not on flavor.

Meats and Poultry

Cut all visible fat from chops, roasts, and steaks. Remove the skin and visible fat from chicken and other poultry before you cook it. This simple step can cut the fat content of meat by up to one-half.

New and interesting flavors are achieved and calories are reduced when you sauté meat, poultry, and fish in a little seasoned stock or liquid instead of relying on butter or oil. Our cooks keep a ready supply of stock frozen in the form of ice cubes just for this purpose. This provides just the small amount needed.

But stock isn't the only way to minimize calories when sautéing fish or chicken. Try flavored vinegars for exotic and unusual tastes.

Vegetables

Many vegetables that are usually fried can be steamed instead. For instance, gently steaming onions allows their sweet flavor to come through. If you use mushrooms in the mix when you're sautéing sliced vegetables, you can cut way back on liquid or oil because the mushrooms give off a lot of moisture along with the flavor they add to the food.

Don't sauté vegetables to be used in soups in butter or oil. Do one of these two things instead: steam-sauté them using a little of the soup liquid in a covered pot, or simply omit precooking and let the vegetables cook along with the other ingredients. Taste the soup as it cooks. If it's too bland to suit you, add herbs or other flavorings.

Flour is a traditional thickening agent for soups and sauces, but it adds calories! One flavorful alternative is pureed vegetables. Tomatoes, carrots, mushrooms, broccoli, onions, leeks, and watercress work well, adding body as well as flavor. You can also add one tablespoon per serving of cheese or low-fat milk.

That old favorite, the baked potato, has at long last been accepted as a diet food. Most people know that it's the toppings that do the calorie damage, not the potato itself. Choose from the many good, low-calorie toppings. One of our favorites is made by mashing tofu with a little low-fat mayonnaise, then adding a dash of curry or the sprinkling of an herb. Another way to add flavor without calories is to mash a few drops of Worcestershire sauce and an herb-spice blend into the potato.

Calorie-Saving Cooking Methods

Poaching is an ideal, fast cooking method for vegetables and most firm-fleshed fish and boned chicken. Heat vegetables or fish in three parts water and one part lemon juice. A blend of four parts water and one part soy sauce is nice for chicken, vegetables, and red meat. If you wish, season the poaching liquid with vegetables and herbs.

Spit roasting is an excellent and fun way to cook meats. The slow cooking expels fat. Baste meats with their own juices instead of high-calorie sauce.

Stewing and braising are also desirable methods to use with meats because, again, the slow cooking allows the meat to give off its fat, which can then be skimmed off.

And don't forget broiling! It's a wonderful way to cook meat. Just remember to elevate the meat on a rack in the broiling pan so it won't be cooking in its own fat.

In this time, when the cost of food is high, no one wants to throw out leftover meats. And heating them up in gravies is, of course, not for the diet-conscious. Instead, try placing a lettuce leaf in the bottom of a casserole or pie plate, then putting the meat on the lettuce and covering it with another lettuce leaf. Add a little water to the bottom of the pan and bake it at 350°F until the meat is heated through.

Low-Fat Dairy Products

Some dishes just can't be prepared without milk, yogurt, or cheese. But this doesn't mean you have to forgo them. Our cooks use nonfat, low-fat, or skimmed dairy products, such as low-fat yogurt and cottage cheese, nonfat milk, and part-skim mozzarella, ricotta, or Swiss cheese.

And speaking of ricotta, in recipes that call for it, you can substitute 1 percent low-fat or dry curd cottage cheese and reduce the calories by as much as 50 percent. If you want a smoother texture, cream the cottage cheese in a food processor or blender first. To cut even more calories, you can substitute mashed tofu—a low-fat, high-protein, cholesterol-free food—for ricotta and cottage cheese in recipes. Since tofu is milder in flavor, you may want to add a little more seasoning to the recipe. Taste and see.

We often use Neufchâtel, a soft dairy cheese, in place of cream cheese. It can cut up to 25 percent of your recipe's fat content, depending on the other ingredients.

If you're hooked on high-fat sour cream, try using this instead: Process 1 cup of part-skim ricotta cheese in a food processor or blender until it's smooth. Stir in 1 cup of plain low-fat yogurt. Chill. The fat content is less than one-quarter that of sour cream.

Substitute buttermilk and plain low-fat yogurt for milk and light cream in sauces and soups—either hot or cold. To avoid curdling, when you heat them first mix 1 teaspoon of cornstarch into 1 cup of buttermilk or yogurt. Or you can remove the pan from the heat and stir in yogurt or buttermilk just before serving.

Dressings and Dips

Salads—dieters seem to think they can eat them with impunity when, in fact, they can be among the most fattening of foods. The key is in the dressing. Some of the commercial ones are simply rife with calories! There are many low-fat dressings in this book, but if you like a basic vinaigrette, instead of using all the oil called for, you can replace at least two-thirds of it with pureed cucumber or with plain low-fat yogurt. Delicious!

Snacks for Entertaining

Cheese and crackers are standard company snacks. It's all right to serve the low-fat cheese, but most crackers contain large amounts of shortening. Always check the ingredients list on a package of crackers, and avoid any where oil or fat appears among the first three ingredients. (In fact, avoid any packaged or processed foods where oil and butter are listed in the top three ingredients.)

As an alternative to crackers and cheese, our cooks came up with the tasty low-calorie dips and crudites that follow.

Delightful Dips

Dilled Cucumber Dip

1 CUP   *5 calories per tablespoon*

½ cup peeled, seeded, and   1 teaspoon Dijon mustard
   minced cucumbers   1 tablespoon chopped chives
½ teaspoon cider vinegar   1½ teaspoons dried dill
½ cup plain low-fat yogurt

Combine all ingredients in a small bowl.

Creamy Red Onion Dip

¾ CUP   *9 calories per tablespoon*

½ cup low-fat cottage cheese   dash of ground cumin
¼ cup chopped red onions   dill sprig for garnish
1 tablespoon skim milk

Place all ingredients except dill sprig in a food processor
or blender. Process on low to medium speed until very smooth.
Chill in a small bowl. Garnish with dill.

Pip of a Dip

1 CUP   *10 calories per tablespoon*

½ cup low-fat cottage cheese   1 clove garlic, crushed
⅓ cup chopped scallions   1 tablespoon lemon juice
¼ cup chopped fresh parsley   ½ cup plain low-fat yogurt
¼ cup chopped green peppers   parsley sprigs for garnish

Place cottage cheese, scallions, chopped parsley, peppers,
garlic, and lemon juice in a food processor or blender. Process
until smooth. Transfer to a small bowl. Whisk in yogurt. Serve at
room temperature garnished with parsley

(continued)

Delightful Dips—Continued

Creamy Horseradish Dip

2 CUPS   *13 calories per tablespoon*

¾ cup low-fat cottage cheese
¾ cup plain low-fat yogurt
½ cup crumbled feta cheese
1 tablespoon prepared
    horseradish
2 tablespoons chopped scallions

1 tablespoon minced fresh
    parsley
½ teaspoon dried basil
½ teaspoon dried oregano
1 clove garlic, minced

    Place all ingredients in a food processor or blender. Process on low to medium speed until smooth, scraping down sides of container as necessary. Chill.

Hummus

3 CUPS   *21 calories per tablespoon*

2 tablespoons chopped fresh
    parsley
⅓ cup tahini (sesame seed paste)
⅓ cup lemon juice

¼ cup water
2 tablespoons olive oil
2 cloves garlic
2 cups cooked chick-peas

    Place all ingredients in a food processor or blender. Process on medium speed until smooth, stopping the blender and scraping down sides as necessary. Store, tightly covered in refrigerator.

Appetizing Crudites

Vegetable	How to Cut
Broccoli	cut into florets
Carrots	cut with a crinkle cutter or slice into quarters lengthwise
Cauliflower	cut into florets
Celery	cut stalks to 3 inches, cut fine slits halfway down each piece and drop in ice water for an hour to make fans
Cherry tomatoes	leave whole
Chinese cabbage	serve ribs only
Cucumbers	cut into sticks and rounds (for rounds, peel cucumber if waxed; run tines of a fork down all sides, then slice) or slice into quarters lengthwise
Daikon radishes	cut into strips
Green beans	leave whole; snip off ends
Icicle radishes	cut into rounds or cut into sticks with a crinkle cutter
Jicama	cut into half-moons and sticks
Radishes	cut into roses and drop in ice water before serving
Scallions	leave whole
Sugar snap peas	leave whole
White mushrooms	leave whole or cut off stems
Zucchini	cut into sticks and rounds or slice into quarters lengthwise

Pizza Riso

8 SERVINGS   *143 calories per serving*

This unusual pizza has a savory crust of seasoned rice. It's quick to make because there's no dough to rise.

1 cup coarsely grated carrots	1 teaspoon dried basil, divided
2½ cups cooked brown rice	½ to ¾ cup tomato sauce
⅓ cup whole wheat flour	1½ cups shredded part-skim
½ cup low-fat cottage cheese	mozzarella cheese
2 tablespoons minced onions	

Preheat oven to 350°F.

Place carrots in a strainer and cover with a weighted plate. Let drain for 20 minutes. Pat dry. Combine carrots with rice, flour, cottage cheese, onions, and ½ teaspoon of the basil.

Coat a 9 × 13-inch pan with vegetable cooking spray. Spread crust mixture across bottom of pan and ¼ inch up sides. (For round pizzas, place on a baking sheet and shape dough into 2 circles. Pinch up edges to form a low rim around each.) Bake on middle oven rack for 25 minutes. Then brown crust under broiler for a few minutes, removing before carrots start to burn. (There's no need to cool crust before topping.)

Spread tomato sauce over crust and top with cheese. Sprinkle remaining basil over cheese and bake until cheese is brown and bubbly, 20 to 25 minutes.

Sesame Cucumber Salad

4 SERVINGS   *41 calories per serving*

1 large seedless cucumber	1 teaspoon honey
1 cup seedless grapes	1 teaspoon low-sodium soy sauce
2 tablespoons rice vinegar	1 teaspoon sesame oil

Peel cucumber and cut into ½-inch slices. Cut slices into chunks.

In a medium-size bowl, combine cucumbers with grapes.

In a small bowl, mix together vinegar, honey, soy sauce, and oil. Toss with grape-cucumber mixture. Chill.

Yard-Long Beans with Oyster Sauce

4 SERVINGS   *146 calories per serving*

The Chinese consider it bad luck to cut these beans. So they eat them bite by bite, using chopsticks to hold up the length.

5 dried shiitake mushrooms (1
    to 2 inches each)
1 slice ginger root
¾ pound yard-long beans
2 tablespoons oyster sauce*
1 tablespoon *mirin** (sweet rice
    vinegar)

1 teaspoon cornstarch
2 teaspoons vegetable oil
2 cloves garlic
    dash of sesame oil
1 tablespoon sesame seeds

Rinse mushrooms and remove stems. Soak in boiling water to cover for 15 to 20 minutes, or until soft. (Weight mushrooms down if they float.)

Place ginger into a large saucepan containing about an inch of water. Cover and bring to a boil. Place beans in a steamer basket. Add to the pan, cover, and steam for 2 to 3 minutes. Remove beans and set aside.

Remove mushrooms from water. Pat dry and cut into slivers. Combine oyster sauce, *mirin*, and cornstarch in a cup and stir until smooth. Set aside.

Heat a wok over medium-high heat. Add vegetable oil and garlic and stir-fry for about 30 seconds. Discard garlic. Quickly add beans and mushrooms. Stir-fry for 2 minutes. Make a space in the bottom of the wok and add oyster sauce mixture. Quickly stir until thick. (This won't take long, so be careful not to burn the sauce.) Toss beans and mushrooms to coat with sauce. Sprinkle with a little sesame oil and toss again. Arrange on a round platter in a nest shape. Sprinkle with sesame seeds.

*Available in Oriental markets.

Shrimp in Chili Sauce

4 SERVINGS   *186 calories per serving*

Serve this tangy, aromatic entree over cooked rice.

½ cup minced onions
2 cloves garlic, minced
1 tablespoon minced fresh
    coriander or parsley
¼ cup chicken stock
1¼ pounds large shrimp, shelled
    and deveined

½ cup Mexican salsa or taco
    sauce
1 teaspoon chili powder
¼ teaspoon ground cumin

In a medium-size saucepan, sauté onions, garlic, and coriander or parsley in stock for 2 to 3 minutes. Add shrimp and continue cooking until shrimp just turn pink, about 4 to 8 minutes, depending on size. Don't overcook.

In a small bowl, combine salsa or taco sauce, chili powder, and cumin. Add to shrimp and heat through.

Shrimply Delicious

32 HORS D'OEUVRES   *7–8 calories per hors d'oeuvre*

Serve these tidbits plain, with a squeeze of lemon juice, or dipped in cocktail sauce.

32 snow peas, ends removed
32 shrimp, shelled and deveined

Bring a large pot of water to a boil. Add snow peas and blanch for 2 minutes. Remove with slotted spoon and drain on paper towels.

Add shrimp to water. After water returns to a boil, cook shrimp for 4 minutes. Remove with a slotted spoon and drain on paper towels.

Wrap each snow pea around a shrimp and secure with a food pick. Chill.

Sole and Salmon Roulades

12 ROULADES   *50 calories per roulade*

5 ounces boned and skinned
    fresh pink salmon, cut into
    1-inch chunks
2 tablespoons beaten egg or egg
    substitute
1 teaspoon Dijon mustard

½ teaspoon minced fresh dill
1 pound sole or flounder fillets
    (about 6)
dill sprigs for garnish
Dijon mustard to serve at the
    table

In a food processor, blend salmon, egg, 1 teaspoon mustard, and dill. Process until you have a well-combined thick paste.

Set a steamer basket in a pot containing about an inch of water. Bring water to a boil.

Cut each fillet in half lengthwise along its natural crease. Place 1 teaspoon of salmon paste at the tip of each fillet. Roll up to enclose filling and place fillets, seam side down, in steamer basket. Cover pot and steam for 4 minutes. Serve garnished with dill and with additional mustard on the side.

South India Poached Chicken

4 SERVINGS   *155 calories per serving*

1 cup water
1 cup vinegar
2 thin slices ginger root, divided
1 clove garlic, minced

2 whole chicken breasts, halved,
    boned, and skinned
½ cup plain low-fat yogurt
1 tablespoon minced orange
    peel

In a large skillet, combine water, vinegar, 1 slice of the ginger, garlic, and chicken. Simmer, covered, for about 25 minutes. Remove chicken and keep warm. Strain poaching liquid, reserving it.

In a small bowl, combine yogurt and orange peel with 2 tablespoons of the poaching liquid. Mince remaining ginger and stir into sauce. Serve over chicken.

Baked Potatoes with Creamy Mustard Topping

2 SERVINGS   *100 calories per serving*

2 medium-size baking potatoes
½ cup low-fat cottage cheese
¼ cup skim milk

1 tablespoon Dijon mustard
1 tablespoon chopped scallions

Bake potatoes until tender.

Combine cottage cheese, milk, mustard, and scallions in a blender. Puree until satin smooth.

Split potatoes and spoon topping over halves.

Baliñas

12 HORS D'OEUVRES   *16-18 calories per hors d'oeuvre*

⅓ cup chopped cooked white fish
¼ cup shredded Muenster cheese
1 shallot, minced
½ teaspoon dried marjoram
½ teaspoon dried thyme

2 teaspoons toasted wheat germ
1 teaspoon minced fresh parsley
2 radishes, thinly sliced
12 watercress leaves

Mash fish and cheese together in a food processor or in a blender on medium speed.

Place mixture into a small bowl and mix in shallots, marjoram, and thyme. Form 12 balls and roll each in wheat germ and parsley to cover. Spear each ball with a food pick and add a radish slice and watercress leaf.

> VARIATIONS: Use any chopped cooked or canned fish instead of white fish. Chopped cooked chicken is delicious, too.

Buttermilk Drop Biscuits

1½ DOZEN BISCUITS   *58 calories per biscuit*

1 cup whole wheat flour
1 cup unbleached white flour
2 teaspoons baking powder
1 teaspoon cream of tartar

1 tablespoon minced fresh dill
   (other herbs such as thyme,
   basil, oregano, or rosemary
   may be substituted)
1⅓ cups buttermilk

Preheat oven to 450°F.

In a medium-size bowl, mix together whole wheat flour, unbleached white flour, baking powder, cream of tartar, and dill. Add buttermilk and mix batter with a large rubber spatula using as few strokes as possible.

Drop tablespoonfuls of batter onto a baking sheet that's been sprayed with vegetable cooking spray and bake for about 14 minutes.

VARIATIONS: When adding herbs, toss in 1 to 2 tablespoons of grated carrots or finely minced scallions. Or omit herbs and add 2 tablespoons chopped dried fruit.

Chicken Gumbo

6 SERVINGS   *119 calories per serving*

Frozen greens and okra also work well in this recipe.

5 cups water	½ cup minced onions
½ pound fresh collard greens or mustard greens	½ cup minced celery
	¼ cup minced scallions
1 pound fresh spinach, shredded	¼ cup whole wheat flour
	¾ cup coarsely chopped tomatoes
6 sprigs parsley	2 cloves garlic, minced
1 bay leaf	½ teaspoon dried thyme
1 pound boneless, skinless chicken breast, cut into 1-inch pieces	¼ teaspoon cayenne pepper
	¼ teaspoon ground allspice
½ pound fresh okra, cut into 1-inch pieces	½ teaspoon soy sauce

In a medium-size saucepan, bring water to a boil. Drop in greens and spinach and reduce heat to low. Tie parsley and bay leaf together and add to pan. Cook, partially covered, for 1 hour, or until greens are tender. Discard bay leaf and parsley. Press greens firmly through a sieve over a bowl. Strain cooking liquid and reserve. Puree greens in a food processor or blender.

In a medium-size skillet coated with vegetable cooking spray, sauté chicken until browned, adding about ¼ cup of the cooking liquid if necessary to prevent scorching. Remove chicken and sauté okra in ¼ cup of the cooking liquid until white threads disappear. Remove okra, add another ¼ cup of the cooking liquid, and sauté the onions, celery, and scallions until wilted.

In a medium-size saucepan, make a paste with flour and ½ cup cooking liquid, heating slowly and stirring. Whisk vigorously to make mixture free of lumps. Add remaining cooking liquid, stirring until combined. Whisk, if necessary. Add reserved greens, chicken, okra, onions, celery, scallions, tomatoes, garlic, thyme, cayenne, allspice, and soy sauce. Bring to a boil, reduce heat to low, and simmer, partially covered, for 30 minutes.

Cilantro Tomatoes

24 HORS D'OEUVRES *15 calories per hors d'oeuvre*

These are lovely hors d'oeuvres to serve when you and your guests are weight watching (and who isn't?).

24 cherry tomatoes
⅔ cup low-fat cottage cheese
1 small scallion, minced
1 tablespoon minced fresh
    cilantro or parsley
½ clove garlic

½ teaspoon dried basil
¼ teaspoon dried marjoram
    dash of curry powder
    fresh spinach leaves for garnish
    parsley sprigs for garnish

Cut top third of cherry tomatoes almost through to form a lid. Carefully scoop out seeds with a melon baller and discard them. Drain hollowed out cherry tomatoes upside down on a kitchen towel while preparing filling.

In a small bowl, mix together cottage cheese, scallions, and cilantro or parsley. Add garlic by pushing it through a garlic press into the bowl. Add basil, marjoram, and curry and stir well. Use a small spoon to fill cherry tomatoes with cheese mixture. Use enough of the cheese so the lids are held partly opened and stuffing is visible. Chill.

Arrange spinach leaves on a serving platter and set stuffed tomatoes on top. Garnish with parsley sprigs and serve immediately.

Diamond Head Chicken with Pineapple

4 SERVINGS   *157 calories per serving*

This Hawaiian specialty is served in a pineapple shell.

½ cup pineapple juice
3 tablespoons cider vinegar
2 tablespoons low-sodium soy
  sauce
2 tablespoons minced onions
1 teaspoon minced ginger root
1 clove garlic, minced

¾ pound boneless, skinless
  chicken breasts
1 ripe pineapple
1 teaspoon cornstarch
1 green pepper, cut into thin
  strips
1 sweet red pepper, cut into thin
  strips

In a medium-size bowl, combine juice, vinegar, soy sauce, onions, ginger, and garlic. Slice chicken into bite-size pieces, add to bowl, and let marinate for 4 hours.

Cut pineapple in half lengthwise, leaving the top of each half intact. Reserve one half for another use. With a sharp knife, loosen flesh from the other half, scoop out with a spoon, and cut into ½-inch strips. Set aside pineapple and shell.

Drain marinade from chicken, reserving ½ cup. Heat a wok or large nonstick skillet over medium-high heat. Add 3 tablespoons of marinade. Stir-fry chicken until just brown. Don't overcook. Remove from pan. Add the rest of reserved marinade plus cornstarch to pan. Stir constantly until thick, about 20 seconds. Quickly add green and red peppers, pineapple, and chicken. Toss to coat with sauce, and remove from heat. Pile into pineapple shell and serve immediately.

Eggplant Soup with Tiny Pasta

8 SERVINGS   *120 calories per serving*

 1 medium-size onion, minced
 2 cloves garlic, minced
 ¼ cup minced celery leaf
 1 teaspoon olive oil
 4 cups cubed peeled eggplant
12 tomatoes, peeled and
    quartered
3½ cups chicken stock

 ½ teaspoon fresh thyme or
    ¼ teaspoon dried thyme
 ½ teaspoon fresh rosemary,
    crushed, or ¼ teaspoon
    dried rosemary
 1 cup orzo or tiny pasta of your
    choice, cooked
    grated Parmesan cheese, to
    sprinkle

In a large soup pot, sauté onions, garlic, and celery leaf in oil for 3 minutes. Add eggplant and tomatoes, cover, and let simmer for 10 minutes. Add chicken stock, thyme, and rosemary and continue to simmer for about 20 minutes more. Add orzo and serve with cheese to sprinkle at the table.

Yogurt and Cucumber Raita

4 SERVINGS   *85 calories per serving*

 1 large cucumber
 2 tablespoons minced red
    onions
 1 tomato, chopped
 2 tablespoons minced fresh
    coriander

 1 teaspoon ground cumin
 ⅛ teaspoon cayenne pepper
 2 cups plain low-fat yogurt

Peel, seed, and coarsely shred cucumber. Combine cucumbers and onions in a medium-size bowl. Let stand 5 minutes. Gently squeeze pulp, a handful at a time, to remove excess moisture. Return to bowl and add tomatoes and coriander, tossing lightly to combine.

Toast cumin in a small skillet over low heat for 30 seconds, stirring to prevent scorching. Add cumin and cayenne to yogurt. Stir yogurt into cucumber mixture.

Chill before serving.

Ginger-Pickled Vegetables

4 SERVINGS   *25 calories per serving*

1 cup thinly sliced cabbage
1 medium-size cucumber, diced
1 sliced daikon radish, cut into
     julienne strips
1 1-inch cube ginger root

½ cup rice vinegar
2 tablespoons *mirin** (sweet rice
     vinegar)
¼ cup water

In a large bowl, combine cabbage, cucumbers, and daikon. Cut ginger into very thin strips. Add to vegetables.

In a small bowl, mix together rice vinegar, *mirin*, and water. Pour over vegetables and toss to coat. Chill before serving.

*Available in Oriental markets.

Herb-Poached Shrimp

10 SERVINGS   *78 calories per serving*

2 cups court bouillon or
     chicken stock
2 cloves garlic, minced
1 tablespoon rosemary,
     crumbled
1¼ pounds shrimp, shelled and
     deveined

1 tablespoon lime juice
1 tablespoon apple juice
1 tablespoon minced
     fresh parsley
¼ teaspoon paprika

In a medium-size saucepan, combine bouillon, garlic, and rosemary. Cover and bring to a boil. Add shrimp, reduce heat, and simmer covered, for 3 to 5 minutes, or until shrimp are pink. Do not overcook.

Drain shrimp and run under cold water to stop cooking.

In a small saucepan, combine lime juice, apple juice, parsley, and paprika and heat through. Toss shrimp with juice mixture and serve immediately.

Iced Rhubarb-Strawberry Soup

8 SERVINGS   *57 calories per serving*

4 cups coarsely chopped fresh
   rhubarb
2 cups apple juice
2 cups sliced fresh strawberries

plain low-fat yogurt for garnish
sliced fresh strawberries for
   garnish

In a large saucepan, combine rhubarb and apple juice. Cover and simmer for about 45 minutes. The longer the rhubarb cooks, the sweeter it becomes. Stir occasionally to prevent scorching.

Puree rhubarb with 2 cups strawberries in a food processor or blender. Chill soup for several hours and stir well before serving. Garnish with a dollop of yogurt and sliced strawberries.

Italian Orchard Acorn Squash

2 SERVINGS   *138 calories per serving*

1 medium-size acorn squash
¾ cup unsweetened applesauce

1 teaspooon grated Parmesan
   cheese

Cut squash in half, remove and discard seeds and stringy membranes, and bake at 375°F for 40 to 45 minutes.

Fill squash with applesauce, brushing a bit of applesauce over exposed edges. Sprinkle with cheese and broil 4 to 5 minutes.

VARIATIONS: Use ⅛ teaspoon ground cinnamon or grated nutmeg instead of cheese.

Italian Wedding Soup

8 SERVINGS · *171-182 calories per serving*

This traditional Italian specialty was christened "Italian Wedding Soup"
because the beaten eggs appear to form a bridal veil over its top.

8 to 10 cups vegetable stock
½ pound lean ground beef
1 tablespoon minced fresh
 parsley
1 tablespoon minced onions
¼ teaspoon minced garlic
¼ cup whole grain bread crumbs
5 tablespoons skim milk
1 pound fresh escarole, washed

2 medium-size carrots, coarsely
 chopped
1 stalk celery, coarsely chopped
2 eggs, beaten with 2 tablespoons cold water
1 tablespoon chopped fresh
 parsley
1 hard-cooked egg, sliced, for
 garnish

Preheat oven to 375°F.

In a 6-quart saucepan, bring stock to a slow boil. Simmer,
covered, while preparing meatballs.

In a medium-size bowl, combine ground beef, parsley,
onions, garlic, bread crumbs, and milk. Mix well. Using your
hands, roll into 1-inch balls. Place on a broiler pan and bake at
375°F until browned, about 25 minutes. Remove from pan and
set aside.

Steam escarole until tender, about 5 minutes. Coarsely chop.

Add carrots and celery to stock. Simmer until vegetables
are tender, about 20 minutes.

Add meatballs and escarole to stock. Heat through. Add
eggs, stirring until eggs are set, about 20 seconds. Turn off
heat. Serve with parsley sprinkled on top and garnished with
egg slices.

Jamaican Chicken

4 SERVINGS   *119 calories per serving*

Stir-frying without oil makes this a low-calorie Caribbean feast.

⅓ cup chicken stock
2 tablespoons low-sodium soy
   sauce
1 thin slice ginger root
1 bay leaf
1 clove garlic, halved
¼ teaspoon ground allspice
¾ pound boneless, skinless
   chicken breasts, cut into
   ¼-inch strips

½ cup sliced fresh mushrooms
½ cup thinly sliced sweet red
   peppers
⅓ cup sliced celery
1 teaspoon cornstarch
1 teaspoon honey

In a large mixing bowl, combine stock, soy sauce, ginger, bay leaf, garlic, and allspice. Add chicken, stir well, and marinate in the refrigerator for at least 4 hours, stirring several times. Remove chicken from bowl and reserve marinade.

Coat a wok or large nonstick skillet with vegetable cooking spray and heat over medium-high heat, then stir-fry chicken for 3 to 5 minutes, adding a bit of marinade if necessary to prevent scorching. Remove chicken and drain on paper towels. Wipe pan clean.

Reheat pan and sauté mushrooms, peppers, and celery with 1 tablespoon of marinade over medium-high heat for 1 minute. Remove vegetables.

In a small bowl, combine ¼ cup marinade with cornstarch and honey. Return pan to medium-high heat and add the sauce. Stir until thickened and shiny. Add chicken and vegetables. Toss to coat with sauce. Serve immediately.

Spanakorizo

4 SERVINGS   *210 calories per serving*

Greek spinach and rice—a main dish and vegetable in one!

¼ cup minced onions
1 tablespoon chicken stock
1 pound fresh spinach, chopped
2½ cups cooked brown rice
½ cup low-fat cottage cheese
¼ cup shredded sharp cheddar cheese

1 egg, beaten, or ¼ cup egg substitute
1 tablespoon minced fresh dill or 1½ teaspoons dried dill
1 tablespoon minced fresh parsley

Preheat oven to 375°F.

In a large nonstick skillet, cook onions in stock until wilted. Add spinach and cook over low heat, stirring constantly, until wilted and all liquid has evaporated.

In a large bowl, combine rice, cottage cheese, cheddar cheese, egg, dill, and parsley. Fold in spinach mixture.

Coat a 1-quart casserole with vegetable cooking spray. Turn rice mixture into casserole and bake for 20 to 25 minutes, or until top is slightly golden.

Tangy Roasted Peppers

8 TO 10 SERVINGS   *72-57 calories per serving*

4 large sweet red, green, or   1 teaspoon Dijon mustard
   yellow peppers   ¼ teaspoon dried basil
3 tablespoons vegetable oil
2 tablespoons balsamic or white
   wine vinegar

Broil peppers about 6 inches from heat, turning until skin is blistered on all sides. Wrap in a kitchen towel for 10 minutes. Peel peppers and remove seeds and stems. Blot dry with paper towels. Cut lengthwise into 1-inch strips and place in a shallow bowl.

In a cup, whisk together oil, vinegar, mustard, and basil. Pour over peppers. Toss to coat lightly. Allow peppers to marinate for several hours.

Vegetable Paella

3 SERVINGS   *171 calories per serving*

3 tablespoons to ¼ cup chicken   1 cup green beans, cut into
   stock or vegetable stock   1-inch pieces
½ to 1 teaspoon turmeric   1 tablespoon freshly grated
2 cups cooked brown rice   Parmesan cheese
1 cup fresh broccoli florets   1 tablespoon minced fresh
2 carrots, cut into thin strips   parsley for garnish

In a paella pan or medium-size saucepan, heat 3 tablespoons stock. Add turmeric and rice, stirring until rice is golden.

Add broccoli, carrots, beans, and cheese and cook until vegetables are tender but crisp, about 3 to 5 minutes, adding more stock, if necessary. Garnish with parsley and serve.

Thai Pork with Cellophane Noodles

4 SERVINGS *245 calories per serving*

Although pork is usually regarded as a high-calorie, high-fat meat, you can still serve it if you choose leaner cuts like the tenderloin and make sure to trim off every bit of visible fat before cooking.

¾ cup cellophane noodles*
5 tablespoons chicken or beef stock, divided
2 tablespoons fermented black beans, rinsed and chopped*
1 tablespoon *mirin** (sweet rice vinegar)
2 teaspoons cornstarch
1 clove garlic
1 thin slice ginger root
¾ pound lean pork, sliced paper thin
1 cup shredded fresh spinach
¼ cup chopped water chestnuts
¼ cup slivered sweet red peppers

In a medium-size mixing bowl, cover noodles with hot water and let soak for 20 minutes. Drain. Cut into 1-inch pieces with scissors.

In a small bowl, combine 2 tablespoons of the stock with beans, *mirin*, and cornstarch.

In a wok or large nonstick skillet, cook garlic and ginger in the remaining stock for 1 minute over medium-high heat. Discard garlic and ginger. Stir-fry pork and noodles for 3 minutes, or until pork is cooked through. Add spinach, water chestnuts, peppers, and bean mixture. Toss to heat through. Serve immediately.

*Available in Oriental markets

Vegetable Pickle

4 SERVINGS   *60 calories per serving*

1 cucumber
2 carrots, coarsely chopped
1 cup cubed pineapple
¼ cup diced onions

½ cup white wine vinegar
1 teaspoon honey
1 tablespoon minced fresh
   coriander

Peel cucumber and slice thinly. In a large bowl, combine cucumbers, carrots, pineapple, and onions.

In a small bowl, whisk together vinegar, honey, and coriander. Pour over vegetables and toss to coat. Chill before serving.

Vegetables a la Greque

4 SERVINGS   *80 calories per serving*

1 pound broccoli, carrots, or
   leeks (or a combination)
2 cups chicken stock
5 cloves garlic

½ teaspoon peppercorns
½ cup plain low-fat yogurt
1 teaspoon Dijon mustard

If using broccoli, cut into florets and trim stalks into slices the width of your finger. If using carrots or leeks, slice lengthwise into pieces the width of your finger and slice crosswise into 3-inch pieces.

In a large skillet, heat stock, garlic, and peppercorns until simmering. Carefully add vegetables (making sure leek layers don't separate), cover, and gently cook for about 4 minutes. Remove skillet from heat and let stand, uncovered, until vegetables are cool.

In a cup, combine yogurt and mustard.

When vegetables have cooled, remove from liquid with a slotted spoon. Serve at room temperature with the yogurt sauce.

No-Meat Dishes

Most of us are striving to cut down on meat in our diets, and of course, some people opt for altogether meat-free meals and become vegetarians. People who get more of their dietary needs from fruits and vegetables seem to suffer less from coronary problems, stroke, and cancer. But isn't it boring to eat this way? Not at all! Some of the world's most inventive and unusual dishes are made without meat.

Spring, Spring, Spring

This is a season for wonderful, nutritious salads! In the greens department, look for mache, radicchio, leaf lettuce, Bibb lettuce, fiddlehead ferns, watercress, sorrel, spinach, arugula, chicory, dandelion leaves, mustard greens, amaranth greens, kale, beet greens, Swiss chard, and endive. There's so much from which to choose!

Accompany them with spring's best vegetables: radishes, asparagus, snap peas, snow peas, new potatoes, scallions, fresh shell beans, and all manner of "baby" vegetables, such as carrots, eggplant, and squash. The earliest of the spring herbs are also making their debuts in markets and gardens. We throw handfuls of parsley—both curly and flat-leaf—into our salads, followed by generous amounts of tarragon, mint, chives, dill, or sage. We love to experiment.

When it comes time to dress salads, don't drown their delicate flavors in an oil-and-vinegar sea. You can often forgo the oil altogether for tasty, healthy, low-calorie salads. And remember that a little vinegar goes a long way. Use just enough dressing to lightly coat and flavor your vegetables. In general, a tablespoon or two is sufficient for four servings.

Mid-Winter No-Meat Meals

Take advantage of winter's earthier offerings, namely beans, grains, and the richly hued, highly flavored root vegetables. They have remarkable taste and textural surprises. Select the root vegetables when they're young and tender, and serve them raw or lightly steamed, saving both time and nutrients.

Citrus fruits are another bright note in winter. Use their color and tang to advantage in salads. Or select fresh apples and pears—prized winter fruits. Garnish salads with dried fruits and nuts or use sprouts, then follow with a bowl of wholesome, hearty soup and a chunk of whole grain bread. Presto, a satisfying meal! These wonderful foods make winter no-meat meals equally appealing as those prepared in the sunnier seasons.

Unusual Fruits and Vegetables

Many unusual fruits and vegetables are growing in popularity and have become far more obtainable over the last few years. We love the versatility they lend to no-meat menus. Here's a brief rundown on some of the most popular ones you should try:

Arugula A pungent, peppery, salad green best known in Mediterranean countries that works well with blander greens such as Boston or Bibb lettuce to give salads a zingy taste. You'll find it in many supermarkets and at Italian grocery stores.

Yard-long Beans Popular in the Far East, they look like very long string beans and the bean pods are usually cut into strips and stir-fried. You'll find them in Asian markets.

Radicchio This bitter-flavored Italian red chicory works wonders in salads, and it is available in many markets.

Bok Choy   A chinese chard or cabbage, it resembles celery and is good steamed or stir-fried alone, or added to other vegetables. Many supermarkets and all Chinese markets carry it.

Tamarillo   This New Zealand fruit has the size and texture of a kiwi fruit, with bright orange flesh and black seeds, combining sweet and sour flavors. This fruit is becoming available in most markets.

Guava   It's reddish purple on the outside, white on the inside, and can be eaten raw or cooked (try it combined with pineapple and banana or baked in pie). Guavas are found in most markets.

Passion Fruit   This lustily named fruit has a deep, dusty purple color and often ripens to look uneven and lumpy, but you just halve it and eat the greenish-yellow pulp and seeds with a spoon. This treat is also available in most markets.

Gooseberries   They have translucent skins that vary in color from green to yellow, white, pink, or red, and there are sweet and tart varieties. You'll find them in most markets.

Boysenberries   A type of blackberry with an excellent, tart flavor, the boysenberry is large and soft with a purplish-black cast and large seeds. Most markets carry them.

Everyone's Favorite Vegetable

Well, not everyone's. But the potato certainly ranks high on most people's list of favorites. Mashed, baked, or steamed, the versatile potato can fill you up without filling you out. It's low in fat, high in fiber, packed with vitamins and minerals, and by itself has only a few more calories than an apple. All in all, it has a lot to recommend it. The following are some of our favorite toppings.

Tempting Potato Toppings

❖ Sprinkle with fresh or dried herbs (alone or in combination). For starters, try basil, caraway seeds, celery seeds, dill, chives, oregano, or thyme.

❖ Top your baked potato with plain low-fat yogurt and chopped chives or dill. For a richer topping, drain the yogurt for an hour in a sieve lined with cheesecloth. The yogurt will thicken to the consistency of sour cream.

❖ For a gourmet presentation, lightly sauté mushrooms and onions. Blend about a quarter cup of this mixture into your baked potato.

❖ For added flavor and unusual color, add a cup of mashed, cooked butternut squash to your mashed potato.

❖ For pizza lovers, top baked potatoes with spaghetti sauce, a touch of oregano, and some part-skim mozzarella. Broil to melt cheese.

Apple Rice Salad

4 SERVINGS

2 cups cooked brown rice
1½ cups thinly sliced tart apples
½ cup chopped celery
¼ cup sunflower seeds
½ cup shredded fresh spinach
2 tablespoons apple juice

2 tablespoons lemon juice
½ teaspoon grated ginger root
½ teaspoon minced fresh
   parsley
4 romaine lettuce leaves

Combine rice, apples, celery, sunflower seeds, and spinach in a large bowl and toss.

In a small jar, shake together apple juice, lemon juice, ginger, and parsley. Pour over rice mixture and toss again. Arrange romaine on a platter and scoop one-quarter of the salad on each leaf.

Baked Onion Frittata

6 TO 8 SERVINGS

2 to 3 onions, chopped (about
   2 cups)
1 tablespoon olive oil
½ cup bread crumbs
½ cup milk
½ cup grated cheddar cheese

1 teaspoon dried basil
   pinch of dry mustard
   freshly ground black pepper
2 egg whites, beaten
   Dijon mustard, optional

Preheat oven to 350°F.

Sauté onions in oil for about 5 minutes, or until fragrant. Remove from heat and combine with bread crumbs, milk, cheese, basil, mustard, and pepper. Fold in the egg whites. Scoop the mixture into an 8-inch pie plate that's been sprayed with vegetable cooking spray. Bake for about 30 minutes. Serve warm with Dijon mustard, if desired.

Bean and Pear Salad with Chevre

4 SERVINGS

2 cups fresh or frozen green
    beans
2 cups canned or fresh-cooked
    navy beans
1 firm-ripe pear, diced
2 tablespoons soft, crumbled
    chevre (goat cheese)

Vinaigrette Dressing (recipe
    below)
romaine lettuce leaves
1 sweet red pepper, cut into
    rings, for garnish

If green beans are frozen and defrosted pat them dry with
a paper towel.

Place green beans, navy beans, and pears into a medium-
size bowl. Sprinkle with chevre and enough dressing to
moisten and toss until ingredients are combined. Arrange
lettuce leaves on a serving plate, or individual salad plates,
and top with bean salad. Garnish with pepper rings.

Vinaigrette Dressing

3 TABLESPOONS

1 tablespoon tarragon vinegar
1½ teaspoons lemon juice
1½ teaspoons Dijon mustard

⅛ teaspoon freshly ground
    black pepper
1½ tablespoons olive oil

Mix all ingredients together.

Broccoli-Orange Salad

4 SERVINGS

1 pound fresh or frozen broccoli spears	2 tablespoons lemon juice
3 tablespoons sunflower oil	1 teaspoon grated orange peel
3 tablespoons orange juice	1 head Boston lettuce
	2 hard-cooked eggs

Steam broccoli until tender or just thawed, if frozen. Cool immediately under running water and place in a shallow bowl.

In a small bowl, stir together oil, orange juice, lemon juice, and orange peel. Pour over broccoli and set aside.

Separate lettuce into leaves, wash, dry, and arrange in shallow bowls. Place broccoli spears on top.

Force egg whites and yolks separately through a wire sieve to crumble. Sprinkle whites and yolks over salads in separate bands.

Potato and Blueberry Salad

4 SERVINGS

1 pound new potatoes (10 to 14 small)	1½ tablespoons orange juice
1 cup fresh blueberries	¼ teaspoon Dijon mustard
2 scallions, cut into julienne strips (about ⅓ cup)	dash of freshly grated nutmeg
1½ tablespoons raspberry vinegar*	½ teaspoon freshly grated orange peel

Slice potatoes and steam for 7 to 9 minutes, or until tender. They're done when a fork can easily pierce the flesh. Let potatoes cool, then put them into a large bowl with blueberries and scallions.

In a small bowl, combine vinegar, orange juice, mustard, nutmeg, and orange peel. Add to potato salad and toss gently.

*Available in specialty foods stores.

Carrot Terrine

6 TO 8 SERVINGS

3 onions, minced
3 cloves garlic, minced
2 tablespoons water or
   vegetable stock
1¼ cups low-fat cottage cheese
6 eggs or 1½ cups egg
   substitute

¾ cup minced fresh parsley
¼ cup grated Parmesan cheese
   pinch of cayenne pepper
2 cups steamed sliced carrots
1 cup steamed whole green
   beans

Preheat oven to 350°F.

Cook onions and garlic in water or stock until tender. Transfer to large mixing bowl and add cottage cheese, eggs, parsley, Parmesan cheese, and cayenne. Mix well. Divide into 5 equal portions.

Coat a 4 × 11-inch terrine or an 8½ × 4½-inch loaf pan with vegetable cooking spray. Spread 1 portion of cheese mixture in the pan. Top with half of the carrots. Add a second layer of cheese mixture. Top with half of the beans. Add a third layer of cheese mixture. Repeat layering until all carrots, beans, and cheese mixture are used. Cover pan tightly with foil. Place pan on wire rack inside a larger baking dish. Pour in enough hot water to come two-thirds of the way up the sides of pan. Bake until mixture begins to pull away from sides of pan, about 1½ hours. If using a loaf pan, uncover it for the last 30 minutes of baking.

Remove pan from the water, and allow to stand for 10 minutes before slicing terrine.

Cheesy Pesto Pitas

16 PITAS

These are so filling, you may want to plan only one per person. If you have access to fresh basil, use 1 cup of firmly packed leaves.

1 cup low-fat cottage cheese
¼ cup pine nuts
3 tablespoons grated Romano
  cheese
3 tablespoons grated Parmesan
  cheese

2 tablespoons dried basil
1 clove garlic, minced
2 tablespoons olive oil
16 miniature pitas (3¾-inch
  diameter)

Preheat oven to 350°F.

In a food processor or blender, blend cottage cheese until smooth. Transfer to a small bowl.

Add pine nuts, Romano, Parmesan, basil, and garlic to machine and process into a paste. With the machine running, slowly add oil, and process until smooth.

Do not split pitas. Spread 1 tablespoon of the cottage cheese on each pita. Spoon 1½ teaspoons of the pesto on top of cheese, leaving a border of cheese showing around the pesto. Place pitas in a single layer on baking sheets. Bake for 10 minutes, or until pitas are warm and soft, but not crisp.

Chili and Corn Stuffed Peppers

6 SERVINGS

⅓ cup minced scallions
1 clove garlic, minced
1 tablespoon olive oil
2 medium-size tomatoes, peeled, seeded, and chopped
1 jalapeño pepper, halved lengthwise, seeded, and cut into thin strips or 2 tablespoons chopped canned chilies
2 tablespoons minced fresh parsley
1 teaspoon minced fresh coriander, optional
1½ teaspoons dried oregano
1 teaspoon ground cumin
1 bay leaf
3 cups corn kernels
½ cup cooked black or pinto beans
6 sweet red or green peppers

In a large skillet, cook scallions and garlic in hot oil until soft, about 4 minutes. Add tomatoes, jalapeño peppers, parsley, coriander, if using, oregano, cumin, and bay leaf. Bring to a boil and cook, stirring frequently, until tomatoes are soft and mixture has thickened, about 10 minutes. Stir in corn, partially cover, and simmer about 8 minutes, or until corn is tender. Discard bay leaf. Stir in beans. Keep warm over very low heat.

Cut about ½ inch off top of each pepper. Remove seeds. Steam until tender.

To serve, stuff each pepper with some corn mixture.

Garden Tortillas

12 TORTILLAS

These tortillas are fun to make and delicious for open-face sandwiches and snacks.

1¼ cups masa harina*
1 cup vegetable stock or water
½ cup minced kale
safflower oil for cooking

In a medium-size bowl, combine masa, stock, and kale. Shape into balls, using a rounded tablespoon of mixture for each. Cover balls with plastic wrap to keep them moist.

Place a ball between 2 sheets of plastic wrap and flatten it firmly with the bottom of a dish. It will be about 3½ inches in diameter. Gently peel off plastic and place tortilla in a hot, cast-iron skillet that's been brushed with oil. Immediately flip tortilla to lightly coat both sides with oil. This prevents dryness. Cook until tortilla is crisp and golden, 2 to 3 minutes on each side. Repeat process with remaining balls, keeping tortillas warm and covered until all are cooked. Serve immediately.

*A finely ground cornmeal available at specialty foods stores and many supermarkets.

Winter Fruit Salad

4 SERVINGS

2 tablespoons chopped dried
   apricots
⅓ cup orange juice
2 tablespoons raisins
1 tart red apple
1 pear
1 orange
½ grapefruit
1 kiwi fruit

1 tablespoon sunflower seeds
1 tablespoon chopped walnuts
   dash of ground cinnamon
   dash of ground nutmeg
½ cup plain low-fat yogurt,
   optional
½ tablespoon honey, optional
1 drop vanilla extract, optional

Place apricots, juice, and raisins in a small saucepan and bring to a boil. Reduce heat and simmer 5 minutes. Turn off heat.

Cut apple and pear into slices. Section orange and grapefruit, removing membranes. Peel and cut kiwi fruit into round slices. Place cooked and fresh fruits, sunflower seeds, walnuts, cinnamon, and nutmeg in serving bowl. Toss together gently with cooking liquid from apricots. Chill before serving.

Combine yogurt, honey, and vanilla, and serve on the side.

Green-Thumb Torte

8 SERVINGS

½ cup minced kale
½ cup minced collard or turnip
  greens
2 cups bite-size broccoli florets
2 cloves garlic, minced
⅔ cup minced onions
2 teaspoons olive oil
2 cups cooked brown rice
1 medium-size tomato, chopped

1 teaspoon dried basil
½ teaspoon dried thyme
3 eggs
½ cup part-skim ricotta cheese
1 teaspoon Dijon mustard
⅓ cup skim milk
2 tablespoons freshly grated
  Romano cheese
paprika, to sprinkle

Preheat oven to 375°F.

Blanch kale and collard or turnip greens by putting them
in a strainer and pouring boiling water over them for 3 to 5
seconds. Drop broccoli into boiling water for 2 minutes.

In a medium-size pan, sauté garlic and onions in oil for
about 3 minutes. Transfer to a medium-size mixing bowl, along
with kale, collards or turnip greens, broccoli, rice, tomatoes,
basil, and thyme.

In another medium-size mixing bowl, combine eggs,
ricotta cheese, mustard, milk, and Romano cheese. Add to rice
mixture and combine well.

Spray a 10-inch pie plate with vegetable cooking spray
and fill with mixture. Sprinkle with paprika and bake until firm
to the touch, 25 to 30 minutes. Let cool slightly before slicing.

Greens and Tangerines

4 SERVINGS

2 cups greens (lettuce, spinach,
    cabbage, or kale)
1 tablespoon sunflower oil
1 orange or tangerine
1 cup red grapes
1 tart apple

2 teaspoons lemon juice
1 teaspoon minced fresh
    tarragon, basil, mint, or
    marjoram
    mint sprig for garnish, optional

Tear greens into large pieces and place in a serving bowl. Toss with oil to coat.

Section orange or tangerine and remove most of the membranes. Halve grapes and remove seeds. Dice apple.

Add fruits to salad bowl. Add lemon juice and herb and toss to coat. Garnish with mint sprig, if desired.

Pasta and Peas with Five Cheeses

8 SERVINGS

1 pound whole wheat linguine
1 cup shelled peas
1 cup sugar snap peas
¼ cup grated Swiss cheese
¼ cup grated cheddar cheese

¼ cup grated mozzarella cheese
¼ cup grated Parmesan cheese
¼ cup ricotta cheese
¼ cup minced fresh basil
    freshly grated nutmeg, to taste

Cook the linguine in a large kettle of rapidly boiling water. While it's cooking, blanch the shelled peas and sugar snap peas by placing them in a strainer and pouring boiling water over them for 10 seconds.

Drain the pasta. Turn it into a large serving bowl and toss it with the 5 cheeses, basil, and nutmeg. Add the peas, combine, and serve.

Pasta with Chevre and Fresh Herb Sauce

4 SERVINGS

3 large cepes* (about 1½ inches long) or 3 large button mushrooms
⅓ cup fresh basil
¼ cup fresh thyme

2 cloves garlic
1 tablespoon olive oil
6 ounces chevre (goat cheese)
8 ounces vermicelli or linguine, boiled al dente (7 to 9 minutes)

If you use cepes, cover them with boiling water for about 20 minutes.

In a food processor or blender, mince basil, thyme, garlic, and mushrooms. Remove to a small bowl and combine with oil and chevre.

Turn pasta into a heated serving bowl and toss with sauce. Serve immediately.

*Cepes are dried French mushrooms available at specialty foods stores.

Pasta with Spicy Peanut Sauce

4 SERVINGS

3 tablespoons peanut butter
1 tablespoon low-sodium soy sauce
1 tablespoon rice vinegar
1 tablespoon Chinese sesame oil
1 tablespoon honey

1 to 2 teaspoons chili oil
8 ounces vermicelli or linguine, boiled al dente (7 to 9 minutes)
6 ounces fresh bean sprouts
3 scallions, cut into julienne strips

Combine peanut butter, soy sauce, vinegar, sesame oil, honey, and chili oil to make a smooth paste.

Turn pasta into a heated serving bowl and toss with sprouts, scallions, and sauce. Serve immediately.

Pissaladiere (Onion Tart)

8 SERVINGS

This onion pie with the curious name comes from Mediterranean France. It is wonderful served hot or cold.

1 9-inch piecrust, unbaked	½ teaspoon dried thyme
10 medium-size onions, thinly sliced	½ teaspoon dried oregano
	pinch of cayenne pepper
1 tablespoon olive oil	2 tablespoons grated
2 tablespoons water or vegetable stock	Parmesan cheese
2 cloves garlic, minced	2 tomatoes, thinly sliced

Preheat oven to 450°F.

Prick piecrust with a fork in several places. Bake for 10 minutes. Set aside to cool. Reduce oven heat to 350°F.

In a large nonstick skillet or Dutch oven, sauté onions in oil for a few minutes. Add water or stock, garlic, thyme, oregano, and cayenne. Cook over low heat, stirring often, until onions are limp, about 10 minutes. If any liquid remains in pan, turn up heat and allow it to boil off.

Sprinkle bottom of piecrust with half of cheese. Spoon in onions. Arrange tomatoes over top, then sprinkle with remaining cheese. Bake until color is golden and cheese is melted, about 40 minutes.

Pizza

1 14-INCH OR 2 8-INCH PIZZAS

Neapolitan pizzas are yeasty, soft, and steamy. They're often topped with
fresh, ripe tomatoes instead of sauce.

Crust
- 1 package dry yeast
- 1½ cups warm water
- 3 to 3½ cups whole wheat flour
- 1 tablespoon olive oil or other vegetable oil

Topping
- 2 pounds plum tomatoes, peeled, seeded, and chopped, or 2 28-ounce cans plum tomatoes, drained and chopped
- 8 ounces thinly sliced mozzarella cheese
- ½ teaspoon dried basil
- ½ teaspoon dried oregano or marjoram

To prepare the crust: Stir yeast into water until dissolved.
Place 2 cups flour into a large bowl. Make a well in center of
flour, add yeast mixture and oil, and stir until smooth. Stir in 1
more cup of flour to make a soft dough. Knead dough on
floured surface until smooth and elastic, working in more flour
if necessary. Roll or press out dough onto an oiled baking sheet
until it is about 14 inches round (or make 2 8-inch crusts).
Pinch up a rim around edge.

To prepare the topping: Fill crust with chopped tomatoes
and place mozzarella slices on top. Sprinkle with basil and
oregano or marjoram.

Bake pizza at 375°F for 30 minutes. For a crisper crust,
slide pizza from baking sheet directly onto oven rack during
last 10 minutes of baking.

Potato Curry

4 SERVINGS

2 pounds potatoes, cut into
  ½-inch cubes
1 cup fresh or frozen peas
1 medium-size onion, diced
3 cloves garlic, minced
1 tablespoon minced ginger root
2 teaspoons vegetable oil
1 tablespoon ground coriander
¾ teaspoon ground cumin

½ teaspoon cayenne pepper, or
  more to taste
¾ teaspoon turmeric
1 cup plain low-fat yogurt, at
  room temperature
lemon juice, to taste
1 hard-cooked egg, sliced, for
  garnish

Place potatoes and fresh peas into a medium-size saucepan. Add water to cover, bring to a boil, and cook until tender. (If using frozen peas, add after potatoes are almost done.) Drain and set aside.

In a large, nonstick skillet, sauté onions, garlic, and ginger in oil over medium heat until wilted. Add coriander, cumin, and cayenne. Toss well to coat, then cook for 2 minutes. Lower heat to warm and add potatoes and peas. Toss well to coat with spices. Add turmeric and toss to coat. Cover and heat through. Remove from heat and gently stir in yogurt.

To serve, drizzle with lemon juice and garnish with egg.

Sprouts and Cheese

4 SERVINGS

½ cup garbanzo sprouts or
  other large sprouts
1 cup solidly packed alfalfa
  sprouts
⅔ cup cubed sharp cheddar
  cheese
2 cups chopped green peppers

1½ cups sliced carrots
1 cup chopped cucumber
2 Cortland apples, cubed
  apple cider vinegar, to taste
¼ teaspoon grated orange peel
  for garnish

Combine sprouts, cheese, vegetables, and apples in a bowl. Sprinkle with vinegar, garnish with grated orange peel, and serve.

Roasted Potato Salad

4 SERVINGS

Roasting brings out extra sweetness in potatoes.

1 pound new potatoes (10 to 14 small)
1½ teaspoons safflower or sunflower oil
¼ cup minced red onions
1 clove garlic, minced

1 tablespoon minced parsley
1 tablespoon mayonnaise
1 tablespoon plain low-fat yogurt
½ teaspoon ground rosemary

Preheat oven to 375°F.

Quarter potatoes and pile into a glass baking dish. Toss with oil so that all are coated. Spread potatoes out in a single layer and roast for about 35 minutes. Scoop potatoes into a large bowl and add onions, garlic, and parsley.

In a small bowl, combine mayonnaise, yogurt, and rosemary. Add to potatoes and toss well.

Sesame Eggplant

4 SERVINGS

2 pounds Japanese eggplant
1 tablespoon sesame seeds
3 tablespoons low-sodium soy
  sauce
3 tablespoons *mirin** (sweet rice
  vinegar)
2 tablespoons rice vinegar or
  sherry vinegar
2 tablespoons tahini (sesame
  seed paste)

1 tablespoon sesame oil
1 tablespoon honey
4 scallions, minced
3 cloves garlic, minced
1 tablespoon minced ginger root
¼ teaspoon cayenne pepper, or
  to taste

Peel eggplant. Cut in half lengthwise, then into ½-inch slices crosswise. Steam for 15 to 20 minutes, tossing pieces occasionally. Set aside to cool slightly.

Toast sesame seeds in a heavy skillet over medium heat, shaking pan constantly. Set aside.

In a small bowl, whisk together soy sauce, *mirin*, vinegar, tahini, oil, honey, scallions, garlic, ginger, and cayenne.

Transfer eggplant to a large bowl. Pour sauce over it, toss gently to coat, and sprinkle with sesame seeds. Serve at room temperature.

*Available at Oriental markets.

Stuffed Peppers

6 SERVINGS

6 large green peppers
2 cloves garlic, minced
1 medium-size onion, minced
2 tablespoons olive oil, divided
5 medium-size tomatoes,
      peeled, seeded, and
      chopped, or 1 35-ounce can
      tomatoes, drained and
      chopped
1 tablespoon capers, rinsed

1 teaspoon dried basil
¾ teaspoon dried marjoram
½ cup grated Parmesan cheese
4 ounces mozzarella cheese,
      shredded or diced
8 ounces any small macaroni,
      slightly undercooked and
      drained
2 cups hot water

Preheat oven to 350°F.

Slice tops off peppers and remove seeds.

In a medium-size saucepan, sauté garlic and onions in 1 tablespoon of the oil until wilted, then add tomatoes. Cook over medium-high heat for 10 minutes. Remove from heat and mix in capers, basil, and marjoram.

Mix tomato sauce, Parmesan cheese, and mozzarella cheese with cooked macaroni. Stuff peppers with mixture and place them in a 9 × 13-inch baking dish. Pour hot water into baking dish. Drizzle peppers with remaining oil, cover, and bake until peppers are tender, about 40 to 45 minutes.

Tiny Timbales of Wild and Tame Rice

24 TIMBALES

1 teaspoon butter or margarine
1 tablespoon flour
1 cup skim milk
2 eggs or ½ cup egg substitute
1 teaspoon coarse prepared
   mustard
1 cup cooked brown rice

1 cup cooked wild rice
2 scallions, minced (about 2
   tablespoons)
strips of roasted sweet red
   peppers for garnish
coarse mustard to serve at the
   table

Preheat oven to 400°F.

Melt butter or margarine in a 2-quart saucepan over medium heat. Whisk in flour to form a paste. Whisk in milk, stirring well to prevent lumps. Continue whisking until sauce has thickened. Remove from heat and whisk in eggs and mustard. Fold in brown rice, wild rice, and scallions.

Spray a 24-cup muffin tin with vegetable cooking spray. Fill muffin cups almost full with timbale mixture. Place muffin tin in a pan of hot water. (The water should reach two-thirds up the sides of the muffin cups.) Bake for about 20 minutes.

Remove from water and let timbales cool slightly in the tin. Run a knife around the edge of each timbale to loosen. Remove from tin, arrange on a platter, and garnish with roasted red peppers. Serve with mustard on the side.

Fish and Fowl

In keeping with the new, lighter guidelines for healthful eating, we are starring fish and fowl in our cuisine. The high protein, low fat and calorie content of poultry and fish plus their impressive nutritional value has created an unprecedented demand for them.

The Pluses of Poultry

Poultry is low in fat if it is skinned and prepared properly. The wrong method of preparation can add more than five times the total amount of fat normally contained in the skinned meat, including four times more saturated fat. A half-breast serving with skin that has been batter-dipped and fried contains about 135 more calories than an equal serving skinned and poached or baked.

All supermarket poultry comes dressed, plucked, and ready to cook. We look for fresh birds, which are easily found whole, in halves, quarters, or parts. The parts, especially breasts, can be purchased all skinned and boned.

Young whole birds are more apt to be tender and are a good choice for broiling, roasting, and frying. Older birds do better if they're braised or stewed since the long moist cooking breaks down the stringy meat.

Fowl probably spoils faster than most other meats so it's extra important to know what to look for when you're shopping for one of them. There should be virtually no odor to fresh, chilled poultry and few pinfeathers. Look for soft, smooth, cream colored, moist, but not wet, skin. If the bird is young, the breastbone will be flexible and light colored and the wings will bend easily.

You'll find frozen poultry has a little less flavor than fresh, but the texture is acceptable. Many large birds are sold prestuffed and prebasted. We prefer to stuff poultry with our own homemade stuffing and baste it with stock or butter.

If you buy frozen poultry, check the following: The wrap should form a complete seal. If it is broken, the bird is likely to suffer freezer burn, making the meat dry and tasteless. Look for solidly frozen poultry with no discoloration. If there's pink ice around the meat, or frozen juices at the bottom of the package, the poultry has been thawed and refrozen. Don't buy it.

Up to one-half of the weight of the poultry you buy represents fat, skin, and bone. So, as a general guide, when selecting it, if a whole bird is less than 12 pounds, allow 1 pound per serving; with birds between 12 and 20 pounds, buy ¾ pound per serving; and for birds that are more than 20 pounds, ½ pound per person should do it. As the size of the bird increases, the ratio of meat to bone improves.

A Gift from the Sea

Although truly fresh fish is hard to get in most parts of the country, you can get the next best thing—lightly frozen, thawed fish—even in the Midwest. When you shop for fresh fish (which is what the dealers call it even if it has been frozen) look for tightly closed scales and firm flesh. There is almost no food in which freshness is so important. If the fish looks even a little slimy, pass it by. It will have a strong, unpleasant taste. If you're buying whole fish, the eyes should be clear, bright, and bulging and the gills a reddish pink. As fish loses its freshness, gills turn a faded pink, then gray, and finally, a brownish green. Use your nose, too; you should detect only a mild briny sea smell, not a strong fishy odor.

Fish is cooked to develop its flavor, not to tenderize its flesh, as meat is. Long periods of high temperatures will shrivel fish and dry it out. Cook it briefly at moderate temperatures and it will stay moist and delectable.

Broiling is an excellent method of cooking chunks of large fish, whole small fish, fillets, steaks, and whole fish that are butterflied so they lie flat. And broiling seems especially good to bring out the flavor of fatty fish.

When in doubt, you can always bake fish. This is suitable for all types of fish, and it's the most efficient way of cooking large fish that have been stuffed.

Thinly sliced fish steaks, small delicate fillets, and whole, small fish lend themselves to sautéing. They can be panfried or ovenfried. We don't deepfry because that method adds fat to the food.

Poaching and steaming are the best ways to retain the delicate flavor of lean fish, but these two methods should only be used for the large, firm-fleshed varieties that are not likely to fall apart.

Fish has long been recognized as a dieter's delight, but in recent years it has received some pretty terrific press as a healthy addition to anyone's diet—with its high protein, polyunsaturated fatty acids, and high mineral content. But now, research strongly indicates that an ingredient in fish may have the power to make an important cut in the risk of heart disease. Identified as an omega-3, this fatty acid helps keep blood flowing and lowers cholesterol and triglycerides, two blood fats.

Your Omega-3 Catch of the Day

Common Name	Omega-3 Fatty Acids (grams per 3½ oz.)	Total Fat (grams per 3½ oz.)
Salmon, Chinook, canned	3.04	16.0
Mackerel, Atlantic	2.18	9.8
Salmon, pink	1.87	5.2
Tuna, albacore, canned, light	1.69	6.8
Sablefish	1.39	13.1
Herring, Atlantic	1.09	6.2
Trout, rainbow (U.S.)	1.08	4.5
Oyster, Pacific	0.84	2.3
Bass, striped	0.64	2.1
Catfish, channel	0.61	3.6
Crab, Alaska king	0.57	1.6
Ocean perch	0.51	2.5
Crab, blue, cooked, canned	0.46	1.6
Halibut, Pacific	0.45	2.0
Shrimp, different species	0.39	1.2
Flounder, yellowtail	0.30	1.2
Haddock	0.16	0.66

SOURCES: Adapted from *Journal of the American Dietetic Association,* Vols. 69 and 71.

All this good information has resulted in increased demand for new and innovative fish recipes. Here are some of the best.

Baked Oyster Fritters with Tarragon Sauce

4 TO 6 SERVINGS

Fritters
1 cup boiling water
½ cup bulgur
1 teaspoon vegetable oil
1 medium-size onion, finely
   chopped
2 cups finely chopped oysters
   (about 4 dozen small, rinsed
   well)
½ cup minced fresh parsley
1 tablespoon minced fresh
   tarragon or 1½ teaspoons
   dried tarragon
2 cloves garlic, minced
5 eggs, separated

Sauce
¼ cup plain low-fat yogurt
1 teaspoon Dijon mustard
1 teaspoon minced fresh
   tarragon or ½ teaspoon dried
   tarragon

To prepare the fritters: Preheat oven to 375°F. In a small bowl, pour water over bulgur. Cover tightly with plastic wrap, and let stand for 1 hour. Drain any excess water.

In a large nonstick skillet, warm oil. Add onions and cook until a rich brown. Add bulgur, oysters, parsley, tarragon, and garlic. Cook, stirring, for 3 to 5 minutes, or until heated through. Remove from heat and stir in egg yolks, combining well.

In a large bowl, beat egg whites until stiff peaks form. Fold into oyster mixture.

Coat a baking sheet with vegetable cooking spray. Drop ½-cupfuls of oyster mixture onto baking sheet and bake for 10 to 15 minutes, or until lightly browned.

To prepare the sauce: In a small bowl, combine yogurt, mustard, and tarragon. Drizzle over baked fritters or serve on the side.

Chinese-Style Braised Mackerel

4 SERVINGS

Serve this dish with Chinese rice noodles.

¼ cup rice vinegar
½ teaspoon low-sodium soy
    sauce
3 thin slices ginger root
3 cloves garlic, halved
1 pound mackerel fillets
1 cup chicken stock

1 small carrot, cut into julienne
    strips
1 2 × 2-inch piece daikon radish,
    cut into julienne strips
2 scallions, cut into julienne
    strips for garnish

    In a glass baking dish, combine vinegar, soy sauce, ginger, and garlic. Add mackerel, skin side up, in a single layer. Marinate for at least 10 minutes.

    Bring stock to a boil in a large skillet. Reduce to a simmer and add mackerel, skin side up, and marinade. Cover and simmer 5 minutes. Add carrots and radishes. Simmer 2 to 3 minutes. With a slotted spoon, transfer mackerel and vegetables to a serving platter.

    Discard ginger and garlic. Boil liquid until it's reduced by half. Pour over fish. Sprinkle with scallions.

Dilled Shrimp

6 SERVINGS

Prepare the day before and marinate in the refrigerator until the flavors are well-blended.

¾ pound medium-size shrimp,
   peeled and deveined
2 lemon slices
1 bay leaf
¾ cup water
¼ cup tarragon vinegar

¼ cup minced fresh dill or 2
   tablespoons dried dill
2 scallions, chopped
1 small stalk celery, minced
1 head Boston lettuce

Place the shrimp in a medium-size saucepan with the lemon slices, bay leaf, and just enough water to cover. Bring to a boil, then reduce heat and simmer until the shrimp are opaque and cooked through, about 2 minutes.

Drain the shrimp and place them in a medium-size bowl with the ¾ cup of water, vinegar, dill, scallions, and celery. Marinate for at least 24 hours.

Drain the marinated shrimp. Separate lettuce head into leaves, place on a serving plate, and arrange the shrimp on top.

Fish Soup

6 TO 8 SERVINGS

2 tablespoons olive oil
3 cloves garlic, minced
1 onion, minced
2 stalks celery, minced
2 pounds tomatoes, peeled,
    seeded, and chopped, or 2
    28-ounce cans tomatoes,
    drained and chopped
1 teaspoon dried marjoram
2 tablespoons chopped fresh
    basil or 1 teaspoon dried
    basil

2 cups fish or chicken stock
2 pounds mixed fish and shell-
    fish (cod, flounder, or any
    firm-fleshed white fish and
    shelled and deveined shrimp)
¼ cup chopped fresh parsley
    grated peel of 1 lemon

In a large skillet, heat oil. Add garlic, onions, and celery and sauté until wilted. Add tomatoes, marjoram, and basil. Cook for 5 minutes over medium heat, then add stock. Cook another 3 minutes, turn heat to low, cover partially, and simmer for 20 minutes. Then add the fish and cook for an additional 10 to 12 minutes.

Just before serving, add parsley and lemon peel.

Flounder with Fresh Tomato Sauce

4 SERVINGS

1 onion, minced
½ sweet red or green pepper, minced
1 tablespoon vegetable oil
4 cups peeled, seeded, and chopped tomatoes
1 clove garlic, minced
¼ cup minced fresh basil or 1 teaspoon dried basil

1 teaspoon dried oregano
⅛ teaspoon cayenne pepper
4 flounder fillets
2 tablespoons lemon juice
2 tablespoons minced fresh parsley for garnish

In a large skillet, sauté onions and peppers in oil over medium-low heat, stirring occasionally, until onions are translucent. Add tomatoes, garlic, basil, oregano, and cayenne. Cover and cook over low heat for 5 minutes.

Remove cover and cook for 15 to 20 minutes, stirring occasionally, until tomatoes are very soft but still hold their shapes. Place fish in a single layer over the tomatoes. Sprinkle with lemon juice. Cover pan and simmer for 5 to 10 minutes, or until fish is opaque.

When serving, use a spatula and large spoon to carefully transfer fish to plates without breaking fillets. Sprinkle with parsley.

Fresh Tuna Poached in Miso

4 SERVINGS

2 cups chicken stock
¼ cup rice vinegar
1 tablespoon red-barley *miso**
1 clove garlic, halved
3 thin slices ginger root
¼ teaspoon coriander seeds

1 pound tuna steaks, about 1 inch thick
10 ears baby corn, halved
1 red onion, sliced into rings
1 tablespoon minced fresh parsley for garnish

In a large skillet, combine stock, vinegar, miso, garlic, ginger, and coriander. Bring to a boil, then reduce heat to a simmer. Add tuna, corn, and onions. Cover and poach fish for 8 to 10 minutes.

Remove tuna from liquid with a slotted spoon and arrange on a serving platter. Arrange corn and onions over and around fish. Drizzle with ¼ cup of the liquid. Sprinkle with parsley and serve immediately.

*Available in specialty foods stores.

Herb-Stuffed Rainbow Trout

4 SERVINGS

If you don't have any purple basil, feel free to substitute other fresh herbs. Fennel, oregano, and marjoram are especially fragrant choices.

2 whole trout (10 to 12 ounces each)
¼ cup white wine vinegar
2 tablespoons lemon juice
1 teaspoon vegetable oil
2 teaspoons snipped fresh chives
1 teaspoon minced fresh purple basil
1 teaspoon minced fresh rosemary
1 clove garlic, minced
½ teaspoon Dijon mustard
freshly ground pepper
12 fresh purple basil leaves
thin lemon slices for garnish
fresh purple basil leaves for garnish

Clean trout, leaving head intact. Wash with cold water. Dry well. Place side by side in a 13 × 9-inch baking dish.

In a small bowl, mix together vinegar, lemon juice, oil, chives, minced basil, rosemary, garlic, mustard, and pepper. Pour over trout. Cover and allow to marinate 30 minutes, turning fish after 15 minutes.

Coat rack of broiler pan with vegetable cooking spray. Transfer fish to rack, reserving marinade. Wrap the tails in foil to prevent burning.

Gently bruise whole basil leaves with a spoon to release flavor. Place 6 leaves inside each trout and brush fish with marinade. Broil 4 inches from heat for 3 to 4 minutes. Turn fish over. Brush with marinade and broil until light brown, 3 to 4 minutes. Garnish with lemon slices and basil.

Herb-Steamed Mussels
with Basmati Rice Pilaf

4 SERVINGS

You may substitute clams for mussels, but the cooking time will be slightly longer.

2 teaspoons olive oil
1 cup chopped Spanish onions
3 cloves garlic, minced
1 cup white Basmati rice*
2 tablespoons minced fresh
      oregano

2 cups chicken stock
24 mussels, scrubbed and
      beards removed
1 medium-size carrot, cut into
      julienne strips
1 cup snow peas

In a 14-inch paella pan or other sloping-sided pan, heat oil. Add onions and garlic and sauté for 5 minutes. Add rice and oregano and sauté for 3 minutes. Add stock and bring to a boil. Reduce heat and simmer for 5 minutes.

Add mussels and carrots. Loosely cover pan with foil. When mussels begin to open, add snow peas. Cover and simmer until mussels are fully opened, about 6 minutes. Discard any mussels that haven't opened. Serve immediately.

*Available in specialty foods stores.

Mackerel Salad

4 SERVINGS

2 tablespoons tarragon vinegar
 or white wine vinegar
1 teaspoon Dijon mustard
1 clove garlic, minced
1 tablespoon vegetable oil
1 tablespoon minced fresh
 parsley
2 teaspoons snipped chives
1 teaspoon minced fresh
 tarragon or ¼ teaspoon dried
 tarragon

1 15-ounce can mackerel,
 drained and flaked with
 bones removed
1 cup thinly sliced radishes
½ head Boston lettuce
1 cup firmly packed watercress
 leaves
 parsley sprigs for garnish

In a medium-size bowl, whisk together vinegar, mustard, and garlic. Slowly whisk in oil. Stir in minced parsley, chives, and tarragon. Add mackerel and toss gently. Cover and refrigerate for 1 to 2 hours.

Add radishes to mackerel and toss gently.

Tear lettuce into bite-size pieces. Line a platter with lettuce and watercress. Place mackerel salad on greens and garnish with parsley sprigs.

Oyster Stew

4 TO 5 SERVINGS

This stew is delicious served with whole wheat rolls and a spinach salad.

1 pint shucked oysters with liquid (about 2 dozen)	1½ cups diced potatoes
3 tablespoons water	3 sprigs parsley
½ cup minced celery	1 bay leaf
⅓ cup minced onions	½ teaspoon dried thyme
⅓ cup minced leeks (white part only)	1½ cups skim milk
⅓ cup minced mushrooms	1 tablespoon lemon juice
2 cups fish stock or chicken stock	¼ teaspoon paprika
	¼ cup julienne scallions

Remove oysters from their liquid, reserving liquid. Rinse oysters, rubbing lightly to loosen grit and sand. Place in a strainer to drain. Strain oyster liquid from container through cheesecloth. Reserve.

In a 4- or 5-quart saucepan, bring water to a boil. Add celery, onions, leeks, and mushrooms. Cover pan and steam vegetables over low heat for 5 minutes, or until soft, stirring occasionally. Add stock and potatoes.

Tie parsley, bay leaf, and thyme in a piece of cheesecloth. Add to pan. Bring to a boil, then reduce heat, cover pan, and simmer for 10 minutes, or until potatoes are tender. Remove cheesecloth bag.

Add oysters with liquid, milk, lemon juice, and paprika. Heat over low heat for 5 minutes. Do not allow to boil. Add scallions and serve immediately.

Red Snapper Neapolitan Style

4 SERVINGS

1 2-pound dressed red snapper, head and tail left on
2 tablespoons olive or other vegetable oil
2 cloves garlic, minced

2 teaspoons dried marjoram
1 tablespoon capers, rinsed
juice of ½ lemon
¼ cup minced fresh parsley (preferably Italian)

Preheat oven to 350°F.

Lay fish in an oiled baking dish.

In a saucepan, heat oil and stir in garlic and marjoram. Simmer over very low heat for 1 minute. Pour over fish and bake until juices of fish run clear and it is firm to the touch, 30 to 35 minutes, basting every 5 minutes.

Transfer fish to warmed serving platter. Mix capers, lemon juice, and parsley into pan juices and pour over fish.

Salmon with Dill Sauce

4 SERVINGS

Salmon
¼ cup cider vinegar
¼ teaspoon Dijon mustard
4 4-inch pieces fresh dill
4 salmon steaks, about 1 inch
  thick
1 green pepper, sliced into thin
  rings
1 tomato, thinly sliced
1 scallion, minced

Sauce
2 tablespoons plain low-fat
  yogurt
1 teaspoon Dijon mustard
½ teaspoon minced fresh dill

To prepare the salmon: Preheat oven to 375°F. In a glass baking dish, combine vinegar and mustard. Add dill and salmon. Marinate for 10 minutes. Turn salmon over and marinate for 10 minutes more.

Cut 4 8 × 8-inch sheets of foil. For each serving, place a salmon steak in the center of foil. Distribute peppers, tomatoes, scallions, and dill decoratively on top. Drizzle with marinade. Fold and pinch foil to seal fish inside. Bake 15 to 20 minutes. Remove from foil and serve with sauce.

To prepare the sauce: In a cup, combine yogurt, mustard, and dill.

Scallop Salad with Pineapple Relish

4 SERVINGS

Relish
1 pineapple, peeled, cored, and coarsely chopped
1 red onion, finely chopped
1 small hot pepper, finely chopped
½ cup minced fresh coriander
2 tablespoons minced fresh parsley
1 tablespoon white vinegar

Scallops
3 cups water
1¼ pounds bay scallops
1 sweet red pepper, cut into julienne strips
1 clove garlic, minced
½ cup lime juice
1 avocado

To prepare the relish: Drain pineapple in a colander. Gently toss together pineapple, onions, hot peppers, coriander, parsley, and vinegar. Chill for several hours.

To prepare the scallops: Bring water to a boil, then lower heat to a simmer. Add scallops and poach for 45 seconds, or until opaque. Drain and rinse with cool water. Transfer to a medium-size bowl. Add red peppers, garlic, and lime juice. Toss well to coat, cover, and refrigerate for 1 to 2 hours.

Dice avocado and add to scallops just before serving. Serve with pineapple relish.

Seafood-Broccoli Terrine

6 TO 8 SERVINGS

Scallop Layer
¾ cup skim milk
2 eggs or ½ cup egg substitute
½ cup whole grain bread crumbs
½ teaspoon ground nutmeg
pinch of cayenne pepper
¼ pound scallops

Fish Layer
½ pound sole or flounder fillets
½ cup steamed chopped sweet
red peppers

Broccoli Layer
¼ cup whole wheat flour
1⅓ cups skim milk, divided
¼ cup lemon juice
2 eggs or ½ cup egg substitute
1 tablespoon dried dill
2 cups steamed chopped
broccoli

To prepare the scallop layer: In a large bowl, combine milk, eggs, bread crumbs, nutmeg, and cayenne. If using sea scallops, cut them into quarters; if using bay scallops, leave them whole. Fold scallops into egg mixture and set aside.

To prepare the broccoli layer: Mix flour with about ⅓ cup of the milk in a 2-quart saucepan to make a paste. Gradually whisk in remaining milk. Whisk over medium heat until mixture begins to thicken to consistency of soft custard. Remove from heat and beat in lemon juice, eggs, and dill. Fold in broccoli. Set aside.

To assemble: Preheat oven to 350°F. Coat a 4 × 11-inch terrine or an 8½ × 4½-inch loaf pan with vegetable cooking spray. Cover bottom of pan with fish fillets. Sprinkle with half of the peppers. Top with half of the broccoli mixture. Sprinkle with remaining peppers, then top with all of scallop mixture. Cover with remaining broccoli mixture. Cover pan tightly with foil. Place on a wire rack inside a larger baking dish. Pour in enough water to come two-thirds of the way up the sides of the pan. Bake for 1 hour. Uncover pan and bake until firm, about 30 to 45 minutes.

Spanish Trout Fillets

4 SERVINGS

This dish is equally good using salmon or sablefish.

1 teaspoon olive oil
1 cup brown rice
⅓ cup minced celery
⅓ cup minced onions
¼ cup minced watercress
3 cloves garlic, minced
¼ teaspoon paprika
¼ teaspoon dried thyme

2 cups chicken stock
1 pound trout fillets
½ cup peeled, seeded, and
    chopped plum tomatoes
½ cup cooked peas
    minced fresh parsley for
    garnish

In a large skillet, heat oil. Add rice, celery, onions, watercress, garlic, paprika, and thyme. Sauté for 3 to 4 minutes, stirring constantly, or until mixture is fragrant.

Add stock and bring to a boil. Reduce heat, cover, and simmer for 25 minutes. Add fish and simmer 8 minutes. Add tomatoes and peas. Simmer for 2 minutes, or just until peas are warm. Arrange on a platter and garnish with parsley.

Warm Salmon Salad

4 SERVINGS

3 tablespoons low-sodium soy
  sauce
1 teaspoon minced fresh ginger
  root
1 teaspoon honey
2 cloves garlic, minced
  pinch of cayenne pepper
½ pound salmon fillets
2 tablespoons balsamic vinegar

2 tablespoons minced shallots
1 tablespoon lemon juice
2 tablespoons olive oil
1 pound spinach or kale, torn
  into bite-size pieces
2 sweet red peppers, cut into
  julienne strips
⅓ cup chicken or fish stock

In a shallow baking dish, whisk together soy sauce, ginger, honey, garlic, and cayenne. Slice salmon diagonally into 10 to 12 thin pieces. Add salmon to soy mixture, turning to coat each piece on both sides. Let stand 15 minutes.

In a small bowl, whisk together vinegar, shallots, and lemon juice. Add oil in a thin stream, whisking constantly. Set aside.

Arrange spinach or kale on 4 plates. Divide peppers among plates.

In a large nonstick skillet, heat stock over medium-high heat. Add salmon and quickly cook slices (about 10 to 15 seconds per side). Divide salmon among plates. Drizzle with dressing. Serve warm.

Chunky Turkey Soup with Winter Vegetables

4 SERVINGS

4 cups chicken or vegetable
  stock
1 cup apple juice
½ cup cubed peeled sweet
  potatoes
½ cup cubed peeled turnips
½ cup diced celery
½ cup diced onions
1 clove garlic, minced
1 tablespoon minced fresh
  parsley

2 teaspoons minced fresh thyme
  or 1 teaspoon dried thyme
1 teaspoon minced fresh rosemary or ½ teaspoon dried
  rosemary
1 cup broccoli florets
½ cup cooked baby lima beans
1 cup diced cooked turkey
  finely shredded Gruyere or
  Swiss cheese, optional

Combine stock and apple juice in a large saucepan. Place over medium heat. Add sweet potatoes, turnips, celery, onions, garlic, parsley, thyme, and rosemary. Cover and bring to a boil. Reduce heat and simmer for 30 minutes.

Add broccoli, lima beans, and turkey. Cover again and continue simmering for another 20 minutes, or until all the vegetables are tender. Serve garnished with shredded cheese, if desired.

Polynesian Turkey

8 SERVINGS

1 sweet red or green pepper, cut into 1½-inch strips
1 medium-size onion, thinly sliced
1 20-ounce can unsweetened pineapple chunks

¼ cup apple cider vinegar or lemon juice
2 tablespoons honey
2 tablespoons cornstarch
3 cups diced cooked turkey
3 cups hot cooked brown rice

Place peppers and onions in a medium-size bowl. Add boiling water to cover. Cover bowl and let stand for 5 minutes. Drain well. Set aside.

Drain pineapple, reserving juice. Set pineapple aside.

In a 2-quart saucepan, combine 1 cup of the juice with vinegar or lemon juice, honey, and cornstarch. Heat over low heat until thickened, stirring constantly. Remove from heat and add turkey. Cover and let stand 10 minutes. Stir in peppers, onions, and pineapple. Heat gently until warmed through. Serve with rice.

Wild-Rice Cornish Game Hens

4 SERVINGS

2 Cornish game hens (about 1 ½ pounds each)
2 celery stalks, finely chopped
1 large onion, finely chopped
2 cloves garlic, minced
2 teaspoons olive oil

1 tablespoon dried sage
⅔ cup wild rice
¼ cup slivered almonds
2 cups chicken stock
⅓ cup minced fresh parsley

Remove all visible fat from hens and discard. Discard all giblets except livers. Chop livers into small pieces and set aside.

Dry hens well with paper towels. Place side by side in a large baking dish and refrigerate until needed.

In a 2-quart saucepan, sauté celery, onions, and garlic in oil over medium-low heat for 10 minutes. Add livers and sage and cook for 5 minutes. Add rice and almonds and stir to mix well. Add stock and parsley. Simmer, covered, for 40 to 45 minutes, or until rice is tender and all liquid has been absorbed.

Preheat oven to 350°F.

Loosely stuff hens with rice mixture. Spoon remaining rice into a small nonstick baking dish sprayed with vegetable cooking spray, cover with foil, and refrigerate. Bake hens for 1 hour. Reduce heat to 325°F and add rice dish to oven. Bake hens another 30 minutes, or until juices run clear when pierced with a fork.

Chicken 'n' Biscuits

6 SERVINGS

This all-American combo gets added zip from chili powder. Start preparing the chicken, then while it simmers you can make the biscuits.

Chicken
- 6 whole chicken legs, skin on, visible fat removed
- 3 tablespoons whole wheat flour
- 1½ teaspoons chili powder, divided
- 1 tablespoon vegetable oil
- 1½ cups chicken stock, divided
- 1 cup plain low-fat yogurt

Biscuits
- 2 cups whole wheat flour
- 2¼ teaspoons baking powder
- ¼ teaspoon baking soda
- 3 tablespoons butter or margarine
- ½ cup plain yogurt
- ¼ cup skim milk
- ⅓ cup minced fresh parsley or chives

To prepare the chicken: With a sharp knife, cut each leg at the joint to make 2 pieces. Rinse all pieces, and pat dry. Toss flour and 1 teaspoon of the chili powder into a plastic bag. Add chicken, 1 piece at a time, and shake to coat lightly.

Heat oil in a large, heavy skillet over medium heat for 30 seconds. Then add chicken pieces, being careful not to crowd them. (If necessary, cook chicken in several batches.) Cook chicken over medium heat, turning pieces occasionally, until lightly browned. Pour 1 cup of the stock into pan with chicken. Cover and simmer for 30 to 40 minutes, or until chicken is tender and juices run clear when pierced with a fork.

Remove chicken to a serving platter, and keep warm. Add remaining stock and chili powder to the pan and cook over medium heat, stirring with a wooden spoon to scrape up browned bits, for 3 minutes. Turn off heat and whisk in yogurt. Pour over chicken and serve immediately.

To prepare the biscuits: Preheat oven to 450°F.

In a large bowl, combine flour, baking powder, and baking soda. With 2 knives or a pastry blender, cut in butter or margarine until mixture is crumbly and resembles coarse meal. Make a well in the center and add yogurt, milk, and parsley or chives. Stir with a fork until all flour is moistened. Don't overmix.

Turn dough out onto a floured surface and gently knead for about 30 seconds. Pat or roll dough into a rectangle about ¾ inch thick. Cut into about 12 rounds with a floured 2½-inch biscuit cutter. Arrange on a nonstick baking sheet sprayed with vegetable cooking spray. Bake 12 to 15 minutes, or until lightly browned.

Chicken Breasts with Two Cheeses

6 SERVINGS

2 tablespoons olive oil
2 tablespoons butter or
  margarine, divided
3 whole chicken breasts, halved,
  boned, and skinned
1 teaspoon dried marjoram
¼ cup grated Parmesan cheese
4 ounces mozzarella cheese,
  sliced

4 medium-size tomatoes, peeled,
  seeded, and chopped, or 1
  28-ounce can tomatoes,
  drained and chopped
2 tablespoons chopped fresh
  parsley for garnish

Preheat oven to 350°F.

In a large skillet, heat oil and 1 tablespoon of the butter or margarine. Sauté chicken until golden on both sides, but not cooked through. Place chicken in a lightly buttered baking dish. Sprinkle each piece with marjoram and Parmesan cheese. Top with mozzarella, then with chopped tomatoes. Dot with remaining butter and bake until cheese has melted, about 15 minutes. Serve immediately, sprinkling each serving with chopped parsley.

Apricot-Stuffed Cornish Game Hens

8 SERVINGS

1 cup apple juice
1 cup apricot nectar
½ teaspoon crushed star anise
   (about 2 stars)
½ teaspoon crushed cardamom
   (seeds of 3 pods)
½ teaspoon ground ginger
5 peppercorns
2 teaspoons low-sodium soy
   sauce

4 Cornish game hens
1½ cups chicken stock
½ cup wild rice
1 bay leaf
⅓ cup minced onions
¼ cup chopped dried apricots
2 tablespoons chopped pine
   nuts

In a large, deep dish, combine apple juice, apricot nectar, star anise, cardamom, ginger, peppercorns, and soy sauce. Add hens, cover, and let marinate overnight.

In a 1-quart saucepan, combine stock, rice, and bay leaf. Bring to a boil, then reduce heat, cover, and simmer for about 40 minutes, or until liquid has been absorbed and rice is tender. Set aside.

Remove hens from marinade and set aside, reserving marinade.

Preheat oven to 350°F.

In a 2-quart saucepan, cook the onions in 1 or 2 tablespoons of the marinade until wilted. Add apricots, pine nuts, and cooked rice and heat through, adding more marinade if mixture becomes too dry.

Distribute stuffing among hens, filling cavities. Set in a lightly oiled baking pan and bake for 1 hour, basting occasionally with marinade. If hens appear to be getting too brown, cover with foil.

Chicken Terrine

4 SERVINGS

The chicken will be easier to mince if you place it in the freezer for about 30 minutes first. If asparagus is not available, substitute whole green beans.

2 whole chicken breasts, boned, skinned, and trimmed of all visible fat
1 onion, minced
5 to 7 mushrooms, minced
1 clove garlic, minced
1 teaspoon olive oil
2 eggs or ½ cup egg substitute

½ cup whole grain bread crumbs
½ cup milk or chicken stock
1 teaspoon dried thyme
½ teaspoon dried sage
¼ teaspoon dried rosemary, crushed
5 thin asparagus spears, steamed

Preheat oven to 375°F.

Mince chicken by hand using a sharp knife, or cut it into 1-inch chunks and mince in a food processor. Set aside.

In a large nonstick skillet, cook onions, mushrooms, and garlic in oil over medium heat until onions are tender and liquid from mushrooms has evaporated. Set aside.

In a large bowl, combine chicken, eggs, bread crumbs, milk or stock, thyme, sage, and rosemary. Mix well.

Coat a medium-size terrine or an 8½ × 4½-inch loaf pan with vegetable cooking spray. Spread one-third of the chicken mixture on the bottom. Arrange asparagus in a single layer, with some facing one end of the pan and some the other, over chicken layer. Cover with another third of the chicken. Spread onion mixture on top. Cover with remaining chicken. Cover pan loosely with foil. Bake until terrine is firm and is beginning to pull away from sides of pan, about 30 to 40 minutes.

To serve warm, let stand for several minutes to set. Unmold, if desired. To serve cold, cover top with foil. Place weights, such as cans of food, on top of it to compress mixture. Refrigerate with weights in place for several hours.

Spicy Chicken and Pork with Pineapple

6 SERVINGS

3 canned jalapeño chilies
2 ancho chilies or 1 teaspoon red pepper flakes
1 pound lean pork, trimmed of all visible fat
1 teaspoon olive oil
1 onion, coarsely chopped
4 cloves garlic, halved
2½ cups beef or chicken stock
2 tablespoons fresh coriander leaves
2 tablespoons cornmeal or 1 corn tortilla, torn into eighths

2 whole chicken breasts, boned, skinned, and trimmed of all visible fat
4 bananas
1 teaspoon butter or margarine
¼ cup toasted pumpkin seeds
1 fresh pineapple, peeled and cut into chunks
4 limes, quartered

Wearing rubber gloves, split jalapeño and ancho chilies with a sharp knife. Remove and discard stems, seeds, and veins. Set chilies aside.

Cut pork into 2-inch cubes. Brown pork cubes in oil in a 6-quart Dutch oven over medium heat. Remove from pan and reserve.

Add onions and garlic to pan. Cook for 3 to 4 minutes. Add stock, coriander, cornmeal or tortilla, and chilies. Bring to a boil, then reduce heat, cover pan, and simmer for 15 minutes. Transfer mixture to a food processor or blender and puree until smooth. Return to pan. Add pork, cover, and simmer over low heat for 1 hour, or until pork is very tender.

Cut chicken into 1-inch pieces. Add to pan. Simmer until chicken is tender, about 20 minutes.

Cut bananas in half lengthwise, then crosswise. In a large nonstick skillet, heat butter or margarine until foaming. Add bananas and cook until lightly browned on each side.

To serve, spoon meat mixture onto large platter, sprinkle with pumpkin seeds, and surround with bananas, pineapple, and limes.

Country Chicken and Barley Soup

4 SERVINGS

Treat yourself to this simple, savory soup guaranteed to warm you up, down to your toes. It's a hearty and flavorful remembrance of summer's garden.

4 chicken thighs, skinned
½ cup barley
5½ cups chicken stock
1 stalk celery, chopped
3 small carrots, sliced
1 large tomato, peeled and chopped
2 cloves garlic, minced

1 tablespoon soy sauce
½ teaspoon dried basil
dash of dried oregano
dash of dried thyme
dash of cayenne pepper
2 tablespoons minced fresh parsley

Place all ingredients except parsley in a large saucepan. Bring to a boil, cover, and reduce heat. Simmer for 1¼ hours, stirring occasionally.

Remove chicken thighs from soup. Cool slightly, then remove meat from bones, cut into bite-size pieces, and return to the soup. Simmer for another 15 minutes. Stir in parsley and serve.

Sautéed Chicken with Strawberries

4 SERVINGS

1 pound boneless, skinless
  chicken breast halves
1 tablespoon butter
1 tablespoon vegetable oil

1 cup sliced fresh strawberries
1 teaspoon honey
¼ cup sliced almonds

Place chicken breasts between two sheets of waxed paper and pound them with a mallet to flatten slightly (½ to ¼ inch thick).

Melt the butter with oil in a large skillet. Add the chicken and sauté for about 3 minutes on each side until done.

While the chicken is cooking, puree half the strawberries in a food processor or blender. When chicken is done, remove it from the pan to a platter and keep it warm. Add the pureed strawberries and honey to the pan and stir until heated through. Then add sliced strawberries and fold in gently. Spoon sauce over chicken breasts and sprinkle with almonds.

Quick and Easy

Most people today have hectic schedules. When it comes to food they often resort to take-out meals, fast foods, or commercially frozen dishes. That's fine now and then, but not as a habit. Commercially prepared foods tend to be high in salt; many of them also contain lots of sugar and fat.

But what do you do if you're in a hurry? Our food experts offer the answer with recipes in this chapter that are both quick and delicious. All of the recipes also downplay sweeteners, salt, and cholesterol-rich fats; and they stress whole grains and fresh produce to provide the basis of a balanced diet.

We urge you to experiment with quick foods in this section. You'll find that most of your favorite dishes, even some that ordinarily take hours to prepare, can be made in simpler, speedier versions.

Speedy Pasta and Pizza

Pasta is a perfect example. The very word makes most people think of long-cooking sauces. So when they're in a hurry they reach for a jar of commercially made tomato sauce, quickly heat the sauce while they boil the pasta, then sprinkle the finished product with some grated Parmesan.

What a shame! So many super pasta dishes can be made in a flash. For quick, easy, exotic adventures in taste, try some of the pasta recipes in this chapter. Use eight ounces of uncooked pasta boiled al dente to serve four people.

Pizza is another favorite that most people don't make unless they have lots of time to spend in the kitchen. But we offer a recipe for homemade pizza that is more than delicious, and it's ready to eat faster than the product from a speeding delivery truck even though it's made from scratch. It takes only 20 minutes to mix the dough, assemble all ingredients in one 11-inch pizza, and bake it.

Stir Fast Stir-Fry

One of the quickest and healthiest cooking methods is stir-fry. And the terrific thing about this type of food preparation is that you don't really need recipes. You can combine virtually any meats and vegetables you have on

Mix and Match Stir-Fry for 4 servings

Basic Ingredient (choose about 12 oz.)	Hearty Vegetables (choose 2 cups)	Tender Vegetables (choose 1 cup)	Toppings (choose 2 tbsp.)
Chicken, cubed or slivered	carrots julienne, lightly steamed	bean sprouts	shelled peanuts
Turkey, cubed or slivered	tender green beans, whole or sliced	spinach or kale, shredded	roasted, slivered almonds
Duck, slivered	celery, sliced diagonally	lettuce, shredded	pine nuts
Lamb, slivered	water chestnuts, sliced into coins or quartered	scallions, cut into matchsticks	cashews
Pork, slivered	bamboo shoots julienne	bok choy leaves, shredded	sesame seeds
Beef, slivered	fresh mushrooms, sliced	Napa cabbage, shredded	chopped scallions
Fish, firm-fleshed, cubed	sweet peppers, cubed or diced	watercress, shredded	
Shrimp, medium	broccoli florets or broccoli stalks julienne		

hand to make an appetizing dish.

Yes, the stir-fry method of cooking has a great deal to recommend it besides the attractive variety of colors, tastes, and textures it features. It's a convenient way to compensate for the traditional American meat-as-a-main-event syndrome—complex carbohydrates in the form of vegetables and grains co-star in our stir-frys.

Take advantage of the speed, good flavor, and versatility of stir-fry cooking by using our system that's as easy to use as ordering from a Chinese restaurant menu.

Basic Ingredient (choose about 12 oz.)	Hearty Vegetables (choose 2 cups)	Tender Vegetables (choose 1 cup)	Toppings (choose 2 tbsp.)
Bay scallops	zucchini julienne or cubed		
Sea scallops, halved	cauliflower florets		
Clams	yellow squash julienne or cubed		
Oysters	peas		
Tofu, cubed	snowpeas		
Tempeh, cubed	sweet onion, slivered		
	bok choy ribs, sliced diagonally		
	daikon radish julienne		
	asparagus, sliced diagonally		

Assemble a dish by choosing one ingredient from each column of the chart. You might start with a familiar combination such as chicken, sweet red peppers, mushrooms, scallions, and cashews; then explore something more unusual, mingling slivered duck with carrots, bamboo shoots, dried mushrooms, and shredded bok choy leaves.

To stir-fry, you'll need a wok or a very large sauté pan. (Sauté pans have sloping sides, which you need for quick tossing, as opposed to fry pans, which have straight sides.) You will also need a wok flipper, or two wooden spoons, or a pair of chopsticks and a slotted spoon. Follow the steps below.

Six Easy Steps to Stir-Frying

1. Prepare the stir-fry sauce (page 105) and set it aside, unrefrigerated, while you cook the ingredients.

2. Cut all ingredients uniformly into bite-size pieces, and arrange each category on separate plates near your cooking surface.

3. Heat the wok over medium-high heat for about 1 minute, then add 1 teaspoon of vegetable oil, swirl it around the wok and allow it to heat for 1 minute longer.

4. Add the basic ingredient from the left-hand column of the Mix and Match Chart. Stir-fry by tossing the ingredient quickly. Continue to stir-fry until the food is lightly browned on the outside, which will take 1 to 5 minutes, depending on the ingredient you've chosen. Remove with a slotted spoon and set aside on a plate.

5. Drizzle another teaspoon of oil into the wok. Allow a few seconds for oil to heat, then add your choice of one or more hearty vegetables from the second column on the chart and stir-fry for about 3 minutes. The vegetables are done when they're slightly tender.

6. Immediately return the first ingredient to the wok along with one or more tender vegetables from the third column. Add sauce and toppings from the fourth column. Toss all ingredients quickly to coat them with sauce. Remove from heat and serve immediately.

Basic Stir-Fry Sauce

¼ CUP

1 tablespoon low-sodium soy
  sauce
2 tablespoons chicken or beef
  stock or water
1 tablespoon *mirin** (sweet rice
  vinegar) or sherry
1 teaspoon honey
½ teaspoon vegetable oil

1 clove garlic, finely minced
½ teaspoon minced ginger or
  ¼ teaspoon ground ginger
1 teaspoon cornstarch dissolved
  in 1 teaspoon chicken or
  beef stock or water
dash of sesame oil

In a small bowl, combine soy sauce, 2 tablespoons stock, *mirin* or sherry, and honey.

In a small saucepan, warm vegetable oil. Add garlic and ginger and sauté about 30 seconds. Add soy sauce mixture and bring to a boil, stirring constantly. Add cornstarch mixture and continue to stir until sauce is shiny and thick. Remove from heat and stir in sesame oil.

*Available at Oriental markets.

VARIATIONS:

Chinese Oyster Sauce: Instead of using soy sauce in the basic recipe, substitute prepared oyster sauce. This is available in specialty foods stores and Oriental markets and is a thick and pungent flavoring made from oysters that have been cooked down over a long, slow fire.

Hoi Sin Sauce: Add 1 tablespoon of prepared hoi sin sauce to the soy mixture in the basic recipe and cut the soy sauce in half. Prepared hoi sin is available in specialty foods stores and Oriental markets and is a sweet and savory reddish-brown sauce that's often used to flavor barbecued pork. It's a puree made from beans, sesame seeds, chilies, and spices.

(continued)

Basic Stir-Fry Sauce—Continued

Szechuan Sauce: Mince 1-inch dried chili pepper and add it to the soy sauce mixture in the basic sauce. Double the garlic and ginger.

Sweet and Sour Sauce: Substitute pineapple juice for the stock in the basic sauce and add ½ teaspoon apple cider vinegar.

Five Spice Sauce: Use ¼ teaspoon Chinese five spice powder, available at specialty foods stores and Oriental markets, instead of ginger in the basic sauce.

Chinese White Sauce: Use this sauce to flavor delicate ingredients such as tofu, water chestnuts, and shredded red lettuce. Omit soy sauce from basic sauce and use 3 tablespoons stock instead of 2 tablespoons. Proceed with the basic recipe and add a dash of soy sauce at the end, if desired.

Salads

Good, quick snacks, lunches, or side dishes can be made by concocting a salad. But many of the fine, classic dressings take time to prepare, and we find the bottled dressings unappealing and unacceptable.

No matter what kind of dressing you're using, make sure the salad ingredients are dry. Any moisture on them will prevent the dressing from adhering properly. Always use a large bowl, and toss the salad with a large utensil in each hand. Using upward strokes, toss 30 times, until all ingredients are flavored with the dressing.

To help keep delicate greens crisp, toss them just before serving with chilled dressing. The Food Center came up with these quick-fix dressing suggestions.

Ideas for Quick-Fix Dressings

❖ Rice vinegar with crushed coriander seeds and freshly ground pepper
❖ Apple cider vinegar with freshly grated nutmeg or ground cinnamon
❖ Apple cider vinegar with freshly grated citrus peel
❖ Flavored vinegars (such as tarragon, basil, garlic, raspberry, or blueberry) with freshly grated citrus peel
❖ Red wine vinegar with coarse mustard and freshly ground pepper
❖ White wine vinegar with Dijon mustard and freshly ground pepper
❖ Chicken stock with a dash of soy sauce and freshly grated ginger root
❖ Plain low-fat yogurt with crushed mustard seeds and minced fresh herbs
❖ Buttermilk, Dijon mustard, and toasted poppy seeds
❖ Tomato juice, red wine vinegar, garlic, and ground cumin
❖ Orange juice, rice vinegar, and minced fresh tarragon
❖ Red wine vinegar with garlic, puree of roasted sweet red peppers, and a pinch of dry mustard

Unusual and Quick Sauces

Must quick food be plain? Our answer to that is a resounding "no!" A simple sauce will perk up an unexciting dish, making it special. The sauces below are a few of our suggestions for sauces you can make from leftovers. Try your own combinations, too, using what you find in your refrigerator. Not only is this fast, it provides a use for those bits of foods you hate to throw out, but that aren't enough to make another meal.

Quick Sauces

Sauces	Serve with
1 cup pureed cooked winter squash, ½ cup applesauce, ¼ cup raisins, ½ teaspoon ground cinnamon	lean pork, roast turkey
1 cup pureed cooked sweet potatoes, ½ cup mashed banana, 1 teaspoon minced ginger	poached chicken, lean pork
½ cup pureed cooked carrot, ½ orange, chopped, ½ teaspoon ground nutmeg, ¼ teaspoon curry powder	roast chicken, cooked barley
1 cup blueberries, mashed, 1 tablespoon grated orange rind, ½ teaspoon ground cinnamon	fruit salad, frozen yogurt
1 cup pureed apricots, ½ teaspoon almond extract, 1 teaspoon vanilla extract	bananas, pound cake
1 cup chopped cooked pears, 2 tablespoons dried currants, ¼ cup green seedless grapes, halved	citrus sections, fruit salad

Microwaved Dishes

For really quick, yet healthful dishes, the microwave can be a wonderful asset. Included in this chapter are some tempting microwaved recipes created by our food experts for those especially busy days.

Amazing Chicken Yogurt Bits

ABOUT 30 PATTIES

Serve atop whole grain crackers with a dollop of mustard of horseradish-spiced yogurt.

½ cup roasted cashews
½ cup bread crumbs
3½ cups cubed cooked chicken
2 medium-size carrots, shredded
¾ cup plain low-fat yogurt

2 teaspoons Worcestershire sauce
2 teaspoons Dijon mustard
½ teaspoon dried thyme or tarragon

Preheat oven to 400°F.

In a food processor, grind cashews to a powder. Transfer to a small bowl and mix with bread crumbs. Set aside.

In a food processor, combine chicken, carrots, yogurt, Worcestershire, mustard, and thyme or tarragon. Process until well mixed and chicken is finely ground. Form into patties that are about 1½ inches in diameter and coat on both sides with cashew mixture. Arrange on a nonstick baking sheet coated with vegetable cooking spray. Bake for 20 to 25 minutes, or until lightly browned.

Baked Eggplant Steaks with Garlic

4 SERVINGS

1 large eggplant, cut into 8 round
  slices
1 tablespoon olive oil
½ teaspoon paprika

½ cup chicken stock
8 cloves garlic, unpeeled
8 sprigs flat-leaf Italian parsley,
  chervil, marjoram, or oregano

Preheat oven to 375°F.

Arrange eggplant slices in a single layer in a 13 × 9-inch glass baking dish that's been sprayed with vegetable cooking spray.

In a small bowl, combine oil and paprika, and brush evenly over tops of eggplant slices. Then pour stock into bottom of baking dish, taking care not to disturb paprika mixture. Bake for 15 minutes.

Add garlic cloves to bottom of baking dish and continue baking until eggplant is tender and golden-red in color, about 15 to 20 minutes.

To serve, slip off skins of garlic cloves and smash each clove with flat part of knife. (The garlic will be a smooth, sweet, and nutty paste.) Place a smashed garlic clove on each slice of eggplant, along with an herb sprig.

Cheese and Rice Pie

4 SERVINGS

This ususual pie uses cooked spinach as its crust and makes good use of leftover rice.

10 ounces frozen chopped
    spinach, thawed
3 eggs or ¾ cup egg substitute
1 cup buttermilk
1½ cups cooked brown rice
½ cup shredded Swiss cheese

1½ teaspoons dried dill
½ teaspoon dried mint
⅛ teaspoon cayenne pepper
⅛ teaspoon freshly grated
    nutmeg

Preheat oven to 350°F.

Coat a 9-inch pie plate with vegetable cooking spray. Spread undrained spinach in bottom and up sides of plate. Bake for 8 minutes.

In a large bowl, whisk together eggs and buttermilk. Stir in rice, Swiss cheese, dill, mint, cayenne, and nutmeg. Pour into spinach crust. Bake for 30 minutes, or until a knife inserted in center comes out clean.

Curried Chicken and Fruit Sandwiches

6 SERVINGS

3 cups cubed cooked chicken
⅓ cup chopped walnuts
⅓ cup halved seedless grapes
2 scallions, sliced
3 tablespoons chopped fresh
    parsley

2 tablespoons mayonnaise
¼ cup plain low-fat yogurt
1½ teaspoons curry powder
12 slices pumpernickel bread
2 nectarines, peaches, apples,
    or pears, thinly sliced

Combine chicken, walnuts, grapes, scallions, and parsley in a large bowl.

In a cup, combine mayonnaise, yogurt, and curry powder. Mix dressing into salad. Spoon onto 6 slices of bread. Top with fruit slices and remaining bread.

Elegant Mushroom Cheese Sandwiches

2 TO 4 SERVINGS

2 tablespoons butter or
  margarine
1 cup minced mushrooms
2 tablespoons whole wheat
  pastry flour
1 cup milk

2 tablespoons minced fresh basil
  or 1 tablespoon dried basil
16 asparagus spears
4 slices whole wheat toast
1 cup shredded cheddar cheese

Melt butter or margarine in a medium-size saucepan. Sauté mushrooms in butter for 3 to 5 minutes. Stir in flour and cook 1 to 2 minutes over low heat. Stir in milk gradually, blending well. Add basil. Continue cooking over low heat, stirring frequently, until thick.

While sauce cooks, cut bottoms off asparagus, leaving 4- to 5-inch spears. Steam asparagus. Lay 4 asparagus spears on each slice of toast. Top each with one-quarter of the cheese. Broil until cheese is bubbly. Place on serving plates and top with sauce.

Guaco Tacos

4 SERVINGS

2 avocados, chopped
⅓ to ½ cup thinly sliced scallions
2 tablespoons lemon juice
¼ to ½ teaspoon hot pepper
  sauce

8 taco shells
1 cup shredded cheddar cheese
1 cup shredded lettuce
1 cup chopped tomatoes

Combine avocados, scallions, lemon juice, and hot pepper sauce. Spoon into taco shells. Top with cheese, lettuce, and tomatoes.

Herbed Red Pepper Sauce

2½ CUPS

2 large sweet red peppers,
    chopped
1 large onion, chopped
1 tablespoon vegetable oil
1 clove garlic, chopped

1 cup chicken stock
1 teaspoon dried oregano
½ teaspoon dried basil
½ teaspoon dried savory

In a large nonstick skillet, cook peppers and onions in oil over medium heat for about 10 minutes, or until soft and lightly browned, stirring often. Add garlic and stir for 1 minute.

Add stock, oregano, basil, and savory. Cover and simmer for 10 minutes. Using a slotted spoon, transfer vegetables to food processor or blender. Add enough liquid to facilitate blending, and puree to desired consistency.

Mushroom Cheese Sauce

2 CUPS

Serve this low-fat, low-calorie sauce over pasta.

1 cup cottage cheese
⅓ cup chicken stock
1 teaspoon Worcestershire
    sauce
1 onion, minced

¼ pound mushrooms, thinly
    sliced
1 tablespoon vegetable oil
1 clove garlic, minced

In a food processor or blender, blend cottage cheese, stock, and Worcestershire until smooth. Set aside.

In a large skillet over medium heat, saute onions and mushrooms in oil until soft. Add garlic and stir for one minute. Remove pan from heat. Stir in cheese mixture. Warm over medium-low heat.

Pasta with Eggplant, Pine Nuts, and Sesame Sauce

4 SERVINGS

2 teaspoons olive oil
⅓ cup minced onions
2 tablespoons pine nuts
3 cloves garlic, minced
4 cups diced, unpeeled eggplant
1 cup chicken stock
1 cup cherry tomatoes
1 tablespoon minced fresh parsley

1 teaspoon tahini (sesame seed paste)
1 tablespoon freshly squeezed lemon juice
8 ounces vermicelli or linguine, boiled al dente (7 to 9 minutes)
1 tablespoon chopped fresh mint

In a large nonstick skillet, heat oil. Sauté onions and pine nuts, stirring constantly, until onions are soft and nuts are golden, about 4 minutes. Add garlic and sauté 1 minute more. Add eggplant and stock and cook, covered, over low heat for 20 to 25 minutes, or until eggplant is soft. Add tomatoes, parsley, and tahini and cook 3 minutes, stirring occasionally. Remove from heat and sprinkle with lemon juice.

Turn pasta into a large, heated serving bowl. Add mint and eggplant sauce. Toss gently to coat. Serve immediately.

Pasta with Salmon and Sun-Dried Tomatoes

4 SERVINGS

1 cup water	pinch of freshly grated nutmeg
1 tablespoon rice wine vinegar	8 ounces spinach pasta, cooked
1 bay leaf	12 sun-dried tomatoes, sliced
8 ounces salmon fillets	(about ⅔ cup)
¾ cup low-fat cottage cheese	1 tablespoon grated *locatelli*
2 tablespoons skim milk	cheese

In a large skillet, combine water, vinegar, and bay leaf. Bring to a boil. Reduce heat to very low, add salmon, cover, and cook for 4 to 6 minutes, or until opaque pink. Remove salmon with a large slotted spoon or spatula and let cool. Gently pull fish apart (against grain) into 1-inch chunks. Set aside.

In a food processor or blender, combine cottage cheese, milk, and nutmeg. Process until smooth.

In a large warmed bowl, toss together hot pasta, tomatoes, *locatelli*, and half of blended cheese mixture. Add salmon, remaining cheese mixture, and gently toss together.

Pasta with Shrimp and Saffron Sauce

2 TO 4 SERVINGS

¼ teaspoon crumbled saffron
threads
1 tablespoon hot water
2 teaspoons olive oil
2 cloves garlic, halved
1 bay leaf
1 pound fresh or frozen shrimp,
peeled and deveined

2 tablespoons minced fresh
parsley, divided
2 tablespoons white wine
8 ounces vermicelli or linguine,
boiled al dente (7 to 9
minutes)

In a small bowl, combine saffron and water.

In a medium-size nonstick skillet, heat oil over medium-low heat. Add garlic and bay leaf and sauté, stirring constantly, for 1 to 2 minutes, or until garlic is golden and fragrant. Remove garlic with a slotted spoon. Add shrimp, 1 tablespoon of the parsley, and saffron with water. Cook 3 to 4 minutes, stirring frequently, until shrimp are pink. Add wine and cook 2 minutes longer.

Turn pasta into a heated bowl. Pour sauce over pasta and toss to coat. Sprinkle with remaining parsley and serve.

Rhubarb-Zucchini Conserve

3 HALF-PINTS

This easy recipe can be used as a dip or as a condiment for poultry.

3½ cups coarsley chopped fresh
  rhubarb
1 cup apple juice
½ cup honey
½ teaspoon minced fresh ginger
1 cup coarsely chopped
  unpeeled zucchini

¼ teaspoon freshly grated
  nutmeg
½ cup raisins
¼ cup walnuts, chopped

In a large, saucepan, combine rhubarb, apple juice, honey, and ginger. Cook rhubarb mixture over medium heat until thickened, about 15 minutes. Add zucchini and cook 5 minutes longer. Remove from stove and add nutmeg, raisins, and walnuts. Pour into hot, sterilized half-pint jars. Seal, cool, and refrigerate. Keeps 1 month in the refrigerator.

Salmon and Pasta Salad

4 SERVINGS

1¼ cups whole wheat pasta shells
1 7½-ounce can red salmon,
  drained and flaked
1 tablespoon dried minced
  onions

1½ teaspoons dried dill
1½ teaspoons dried parsley
2 tablespoons lemon juice
1 tablespoon olive oil
1 tablespoon mayonnaise

Cook pasta al dente. Drain and rinse with cold water until cool. Place salmon and pasta in a serving bowl. Combine onions, dill, parsley, lemon juice, oil, and mayonnaise. Drizzle dressing over salad. Toss to combine. Serve immediately or chill.

Salad Bar Sandwiches with Six-Herb Dressing

4 SERVINGS

Dressing
¼ cup plain low-fat yogurt
1 tablespoon mayonnaise
1 tablespoon ketchup
1 teaspoon minced fresh parsley
1 teaspoon minced fresh chives
¼ teaspoon dried dill
¼ teaspoon dried basil
   pinch of dried tarragon
   pinch of dried thyme

Sandwiches
1 cup shredded or chopped
   cabbage
1 cup shredded carrots
½ cup alfalfa sprouts
½ cup chopped tomatoes
½ cup chopped cucumbers
½ cup shredded cheddar cheese
4 whole wheat pitas

To prepare the dressing: Combine all dressing ingredients and mix well.

To prepare the sandwiches: Toss cabbage, carrots, sprouts, tomatoes, cucumbers, and cheese together. Cut off an edge of each pita to form pockets. Spread the inside of each pita with dressing and stuff each with vegetable mixture.

Shrimp Sauce with Cumin

2¾ CUPS

This sauce is great with pasta.

1 onion, thinly sliced
1 tablespoon vegetable oil
1 teaspoon ground cumin
¼ teaspoon cayenne pepper
3 cloves garlic, minced
1 tablespoon minced fresh
   ginger

1 pound fresh shrimp, peeled
   and deveined
2 cups peeled, seeded, and
   chopped tomatoes

In a large skillet, sauté onions in oil over medium heat for several minutes. Add cumin and cayenne and stir for 30 seconds. Add garlic and ginger and stir for 30 seconds. Add shrimp and stir for about 2 minutes, or until shrimp turn pink. Remove shrimp with a slotted spoon.

Add tomatoes to pan. Cover and cook for 5 minutes, then remove cover, and cook until most of the liquid has evaporated, about 5 to 10 minutes. Return shrimp to pan and reheat.

Sweet Peach Sauce

1 CUP

Serve cold as a dressing for fruit salads or as a topping for cakes, crepes, or poached fruit. If you're using fresh peaches, you'll need to cook sauce a bit to thicken it.

1½ cups peeled, pitted, and
     chopped fresh or frozen
     peaches (about 4)
 2 teaspoons apple juice
     concentrate

dash of freshly grated
   nutmeg

In a food processor, puree peaches, juice concentrate, and nutmeg until smooth.

The Ultimate Stuffed Mushroom

4 TO 6 SERVINGS

¾ pound large mushrooms
¼ cup minced onions
1 clove garlic, minced
1 tablespoon vegetable oil
½ cup whole grain cracker crumbs
1 tablespoon toasted wheat germ

1 tablespoon minced fresh
  parsley
2 tablespoons tomato paste
¼ cup shredded mozzarella
  cheese

Preheat oven to 350°F.

Remove mushroom stems by slipping tip of a sharp knife between cap and stem. Reserve caps.

Finely chop mushroom stems. In a large nonstick skillet, heat oil. Sauté stems, onions, and garlic until onions soften. Add cracker crumbs, wheat germ, and parsley. Sauté until crumbs are lightly browned. Stir in tomato paste. Remove from heat. Spoon mixture into reserved mushroom caps. Sprinkle with mozzarella. Arrange caps in a single layer on a baking sheet and bake for 10 to 15 minutes, or until mushrooms have softened.

Tomato Potato Salad

4 SERVINGS

1 pound new potatoes (10 to 14
  small)
1 pound ripe tomatoes, cut into
  chunks

¼ cup minced fresh basil or dill
2 tablespoons olive oil

Halve potatoes and steam until they are easily pierced with a fork, about 8 to 10 minutes. Toss with other ingredients and serve immediately.

Turkey and Fruit Salad

6 SERVINGS

3 cups cubed cooked turkey
1 cup cooked brown rice
1 cup steamed peas
1 avocado cubed
½ cup diced celery
¼ cup chopped sweet red
    peppers
3 scallions, finely chopped
2 ounces sharp cheddar cheese,
    cut into thin strips

2 pears, diced
1 cup seedless grapes
⅓ cup plain low-fat yogurt
¼ cup mayonnaise
2 cups lemon juice
½ teaspoon freshly grated
    nutmeg

In a large bowl, combine turkey, rice, peas, avocado, celery, peppers, scallions, cheese, pears, and grapes.

In a small bowl, combine yogurt, mayonnaise, lemon juice, and nutmeg. Fold into turkey mixture.

20-Minute Homemade Pizza

1 11-INCH PIZZA

The number of toppings that can be used on this lightning quick pizza is only limited by your imagination.

1 teaspoon quick-rise dry yeast
   (about ½ package)
1 cup lukewarm water
1 tablespoon vegetable oil
½ teaspoon honey
1¼ cups whole wheat flour

¼ teaspoon garlic powder
¼ teaspoon onion powder
½ cup tomato sauce
1 cup shredded mozzarella
   cheese

Preheat oven to 475°F.

In a medium-size bowl, add yeast to lukewarm water. Stir in oil, honey, flour, and garlic and onion powders. Mix thoroughly, then allow dough to rest for 5 minutes.

Spray a pizza pan or baking sheet with vegetable cooking spray. Place dough on prepared pan and shape into an 11-inch round crust. Carefully spread sauce over it and sprinkle evenly with cheese. Bake for 12 minutes.

> VARIATIONS: For an unusual topping, spread tomato sauce over pizza and sprinkle with unsweetened crushed pineapple, halves of seedless grapes, and raisins.
>
> To make a pizza salad, bake crust by itself and cover with garden vegetables, sprouts, shredded cheese, and salad dressing.
>
> To make a calzone, place toppings on half of pizza and fold other half over. Pinch seam closed and poke an air hole through the top. Bake until top puffs and browns, about 15 minutes.
>
> For a dessert pizza, omit tomato sauce and top with sliced fruit, chopped nuts, and mild cheese such as low-fat Muenster or Havarti.

Veal in Apple-Lemon Sauce

4 TO 6 SERVINGS

This is delicious served with parsleyed noodles.

2 pounds veal cutlets
1 cup whole wheat flour
4 tart apples, cut into ½-inch
   slices
½ cup lemon juice

1 tablespoon butter or
   margarine
1 cup thinly sliced mushrooms
1 tablespoon vegetable oil
1½ cups chicken stock

Pat veal dry with paper towels. Place pieces between sheets of waxed paper and flatten by pounding with a mallet or the flat side of a cleaver until about ⅛-inch thick. Dredge pieces in flour, shaking off excess.

In a medium-size skillet, cook apples in lemon juice until tender, 5 to 7 minutes. Puree half of the apples in a blender. Set aside. Keep apple slices separate.

Heat butter or margarine in a large nonstick skillet. Add mushrooms and sauté until tender, about 5 minutes. Remove with a slotted spoon and set aside. Add oil to pan. Sauté veal for about 1½ minutes on each side. If needed, add more oil to the pan. Remove veal to a platter and keep warm.

Add stock to the pan and bring it to a boil, scraping the bottom of the pan to loosen browned bits. Lower heat, add apple puree, and cook 2 to 3 minutes. Add veal, mushrooms, and apple slices. Cook 5 minutes.

Wok 'n' Roll

4 SERVINGS

4 whole wheat sandwich rolls, halved horizontally
½ cup chicken stock or water
1½ teaspoons cornstarch
2 teaspoons soy sauce
½ pound beef round or sirloin, cut into thin strips
1 tablespoon vegetable oil

1 sweet red or green pepper, cut into thin strips
1 carrot, shredded
1 onion, halved crosswise and sliced
3 cloves garlic, minced
½ pound mushrooms, sliced
pinch of cayenne pepper

Hollow each roll slightly by carefully removing some of the bread from the inside. Place rolls hollow side up on serving plates. Combine stock, cornstarch, and soy sauce and set aside.

Stir-fry beef in oil in a wok or large skillet just until browned. Add peppers, carrots, and onions and stir-fry for about 30 seconds. Add garlic and stir-fry for another 30 seconds. Add mushrooms and continue stir-frying for 1 minute. Add cayenne, pour in stock mixture, and cook just until sauce thickens slightly, stirring occasionally. Spoon onto rolls. Serve immediately.

Chicken with Chunky Winter Vegetables

4 SERVINGS

A deliciously fragrant one-dish meal that cooks in 10 minutes. Serve with barley or rice.

1¼ pounds boneless, skinless chicken breast, cut into 1-inch pieces	1 clove garlic, minced
	1 bay leaf
	2 medium-size carrots
2 tablespoons lemon juice	2 medium-size parsnips
1 teaspoon Worcestershire sauce	1 medium-size potato
	1 teaspoon cornstarch
½ teaspoon dried thyme	2 tablespoons minced fresh
⅛ teaspoon mustard powder	parsley

In a medium-size bowl, combine chicken, lemon juice, Worcestershire, thyme, mustard, garlic, and bay leaf. Let marinate for 20 minutes.

Meanwhile, pare and then chop carrots, parsnips, and potato into ½ × 1-inch chunks. Combine chicken, marinade, and vegetables in a round 2-quart microwavable dish. Cover loosely with crumpled waxed paper and microwave on high (100 percent) 10 minutes, stirring after 5 minutes.

Remove dish from microwave, and drain accumulated juices into a small microwavable dish. (There will be about ⅓ cup.) Whisk in cornstarch until blended. Microwave, uncovered, on high for 1 minute. Stir into chicken mixture. Add parsley and let stand for 3 minutes. Remove bay leaf and serve.

Cidered Parsnips

2 SERVINGS

1 pound parsnips (3 or 4)   1 cup cider

Cook parsnips in the microwave according to manufacturer's directions. Cut into ¼-inch slices.

Place cider in a small stainless or enameled saucepan. Cook over medium-high heat until reduced by half. Add parsnips. Toss to coat.

Confetti Spaghetti Squash

4 TO 6 SERVINGS

1 medium-size spaghetti squash
   (3 pounds)
¼ cup chicken or vegetable stock
1 tablespoon olive oil
1 teaspoon wine vinegar
½ cup diced green peppers
½ cup diced sweet red peppers

¼ cup diced onions
¼ cup minced fresh coriander or
   parsley
¼ teaspoon ground cumin
1 small clove garlic, minced,
   optional

Cook squash in the microwave according to manufacturer's directions. Split crosswise. Remove and discard seeds. With a fork, scoop strands into a bowl. Toss to separate strands.

Combine stock, oil, vinegar, green peppers, red peppers, onions, coriander or parsley, cumin, and garlic in a microwavable casserole. Cover and microwave on high (100 percent) for 2 minutes.

Add squash and toss, evenly distributing colors. Cover and microwave on high for 2 minutes. Serve piping hot, or refrigerate for 2 hours and serve cold.

Far Eastern Rutabagas

2 SERVINGS

1 pound rutabagas (2 medium)	1 small clove garlic, minced
1 tablespoon soy sauce	dash of cayenne pepper
1 teaspoon peanut oil	2 tablespoons sliced scallions
½ teaspoon sesame oil	

Cook rutabagas in the microwave according to manufacturer's directions. Peel and cut into ¼-inch cubes.

In a microwavable casserole, combine soy sauce, peanut oil, sesame oil, garlic, and cayenne. Cover and microwave on high (100 percent) for 1 minute.

Add rutabagas and scallions. Cover and microwave on high for 1½ minutes.

Five-Minute Tomato Sauce

2 CUPS

Serve over pasta, chicken, or fish. Thin with a bit of chicken stock to make a delicious tomato soup if you wish.

1¼ pounds tomatoes, chopped	½ teaspoon dried thyme
1 teaspoon dried oregano	1 clove garlic, minced

Combine tomatoes, oregano, thyme, and garlic in a microwavable bowl. Microwave, covered, on high (100 percent) for 5 minutes. Puree in a food processor or blender.

Herbed Haddock Parmesan

4 SERVINGS

This is nice served with a tossed salad sprinkled with lemon juice and oregano.

2 tablespoons yellow cornmeal	1 teaspoon dried oregano
2 tablespoons grated Parmesan cheese	½ teaspoon paprika
	2 teaspoons lemon juice
1 teaspoon dried basil	1¼ pounds haddock fillets

In a flat dish, combine cornmeal, cheese, basil, oregano, and paprika. Rub lemon juice into fish, then dredge fish in herb mixture to coat both sides.

Arrange fish in a round 10-inch microwavable dish. Cover loosely with crumpled waxed paper. Microwave on high (100 percent) for 4½ minutes. Let stand 3 minutes before serving.

Maple Mashed Sweet Potatoes

2 SERVINGS

1 pound sweet potatoes (2 medium-size)	2 tablespoons orange juice
2 tablespoons maple syrup	2 tablespoons plain low-fat yogurt

Cook sweet potatoes in the microwave according to manufacturer's directions. Split potatoes to check for doneness.

Remove skins and discard. Place pulp in a microwavable bowl. Add maple syrup, juice, and yogurt. Mash and blend thoroughly. Microwave on high (100 percent) for 1 minute. Stir and microwave for 30 seconds.

Orange-Glazed Carrots

2 SERVINGS

1 pound carrots (5 to 6 medium-
    size)
1 tablespoon orange marmalade

1 tablespoon orange juice
1 tablespoon prepared
    horseradish

Cook carrots in the microwave according to manufacturer's directions. Slice into quarters lengthwise. Cut into 2-inch pieces. Place in a shallow ovenproof baking dish.

Combine marmalade, juice, and horseradish in a microwavable cup. Microwave on high (100 percent) for 30 seconds. Pour over carrots and toss well.

Arrange carrots in a single layer. Broil 4 to 5 inches from heat for 5 to 6 minutes in conventional oven. Toss before serving.

Spicy Beet Salad

2 SERVINGS

1 pound beets (5 to 6 medium-
    size)
1 tablespoon tarragon vinegar
1 teaspoon vegetable oil
1 teaspoon low-sodium soy sauce
⅛ teaspoon mustard powder

⅛ teaspoon ground ginger
2 tablespoons shredded carrots
1 tablespoon sliced scallions
1 tablespoon minced parsley
1 hard-cooked egg, chopped

Cook beets in the microwave according to manufacturer's directions. Plunge hot beets into cold water and remove skins. Cut beets into ½-inch slices.

Combine vinegar, oil, soy sauce, mustard, and ginger in a microwavable pitcher or cup. Microwave on high (100 percent) for 30 seconds. Pour hot dressing over beets and toss to combine. Arrange beets on a platter. Sprinkle with carrots, scallions, parsley, and egg.

Barbecues and Picnics

Eating is an important part of most recreational occasions. Whether it's food for a picnic at the beach, a snack at a football game, or a backyard barbecue, we want the best. Selecting the food is only the tip of the iceberg. Getting it to the plate at its peak of perfection presents other problems. But we think we've solved them.

Picnics

Gone are the days when picnics meant soggy sandwiches and weak lemonade. The picnic has become a more sophisticated affair (for which we're grateful). You'll find our recipes in this chapter not only delicious, but, if you use the tips for packing, they'll travel well, too. A big plus when you're picnicking.

Sandwiches are just one of the types of food from which delicious picnics are made. If you're including them in your picnic, vary the breads. Try whole wheat pita pockets, kaiser rolls, or hamburger rolls. Make some sandwiches with rye bread, others with whole wheat bread, and still others with a good sourdough bread. Cut them into quarters so everyone can have a taste of each type.

Pack moist ingredients such as a sliced tomato, lettuce leaves, onion rings, pickles, and capers in small, tightly covered plastic containers. Add them just before the sandwiches are eaten. This keeps the bread from becoming soggy.

Spread the bread for sandwiches with softened butter, margarine, or cream cheese. Just a thin layer will act as a protective shield, keeping the moisture of the fillings where it belongs. Margarine is better to use than butter because it keeps longer and doesn't require the degree of refrigeration necessary to keep it fresh and safe to eat.

While butter, margarine, or cream cheese protect bread, mayonnaise, sour cream, jams, or jellies are quickly absorbed by breads and will turn a lovely sandwich into a sodden mess in short order. Pack them separately, and spread them on the bread just before you eat the sandwiches.

Tightly wrapping sandwiches and freezing them allows them to serve a dual purpose. Packed in a tightly sealed cooler they'll stay fresh and will be ready to eat in about four or five hours. And during this time, they can take the place of ice, keeping the other items in the cooler or basket cold, too.

Marinated foods are wonderful picnic additions because marinades, by their nature, are also preservatives.

Classic potato salads made with mayonnaise are great picnic fare if you're sure you have the equipment to keep them cool. But to vary your picnic potato salads, try some of the following suggestions by the Rodale Food Center staff. These salads are not only delicious but also keep well.

More Potato Salad Combinations

❖ Chunks of steamed potatoes and carrots dressed with white wine vinegar, thyme, and freshly ground pepper

❖ Sliced steamed potatoes tossed with shredded spinach, shredded watercress, minced chives, freshly grated nutmeg, and apple cider vinegar

❖ Whole steamed new potatoes and minced sweet onions sauced with plain low-fat yogurt, curry powder, and minced ginger root

❖ Chunks of steamed potatoes with minced shallots, chives, tarragon, malt vinegar, and a bit of Dijon mustard

Barbecues

If you associate your grill with hot dogs, hamburgers, and high-fat steaks, you're in for a surprise with this chapter. Rethink backyard grilling. You can cook chicken, fish, leaner cuts of beef, and even vegetables with smashing success. Part of the secret of grilling low-fat foods is to marinate them prior to cooking. Marinades impart flavor and moistness to food, and they also are excellent for basting during grilling.

Instead of buying commercial marinades, make your own nonfat marinades by using stock instead of oil or butter. Add an acidic ingredient such as lemon juice, cider, or a flavored vinegar for meat—or plain low-fat yogurt or buttermilk for poultry. The tougher the meat, the more acid ingredient you need. For heightened flavor, add minced, onions, garlic, shallots, celery, ginger, carrots, fennel, or leeks. Strong spices such as curry, saffron, chili powder, and turmeric offer color and add zing.

Marinate beef, lamb, pork, and unskinned poultry overnight. For more delicate foods such as fish and skinned poultry, marinate about an hour.

Make sure your grilling rack is impeccably clean. Then coat it with a vegetable cooking spray before setting it on top of the hot coals. That helps prevent food from sticking as it cooks. To keep any juices from dripping directly onto hot coals and flaring up, slightly prop up one end of the rack so the juices run down the rungs and off to the side.

For extra taste sensations, try adding hickory chips, mesquite chips, fruit wood, grapevines, tea leaves, or herb sprigs. To avoid flare ups, soak them in water for about 15 minutes, drain, then toss them into the fire. The Food Center staff compiled the following tips for successful grilling.

A Collection of Chef's Tips for Grilling Success

For Chicken

❖ Grill chicken about 6 inches from heat.

❖ Precook chicken in the oven or microwave before grilling so it cooks without burning on the outside. If doing so is impossible or inconvenient, cover the chicken with a foil tent after 30 minutes of grilling; continue to baste and turn frequently until cooked through.

❖ Chicken will stay juicy if you leave skin on while grilling then remove it before serving.

❖ Split whole chicken and other small fowl in the French manner before grilling: Split down the backbone, then turn the bird breast side up. Spread the sides out and flatten with your hands. Press down on the breastbone so it breaks and the bird lies flat. It will now cook more evenly.

❖ Baste chicken every 10 minutes using stock or some marinade. Never baste with a sauce that contains sugar or fat (such as traditional barbecue sauce). It will only burn while grilling. If using such a sauce, reserve for final 10 minutes of cooking or for serving at the table.

For Meat

❖ Grill meat about 6 inches from heat.

❖ Always use lean meat. Trim away any visible fat before grilling.

❖ For even cooking, meat should be uniformly thick throughout.

❖ Larger pieces, like roasts, should be precooked in the oven prior to grilling. If that is not possible, grill for 30 minutes, then cover meat with a foil tent; baste frequently until cooked through.

For Fish

❖ Grill fish 4 to 6 inches from heat, for about 10 minutes per inch of thickness.

❖ For even cooking, fish fillets should be uniformly thick throughout. If the ends are extra thin, turn them under to match thickness of rest of fillet.

❖ Don't turn very thin fillets, such as sole or flounder. They'll cook through as is.

❖ To preserve moistness, grill whole fish with skin and head intact.

❖ When grilling split fish, leave backbone in for easier handling and to preserve moistness.

❖ Fish steaks thicker than 1½ inches are better baked or poached than grilled.

❖ Baste fish frequently with marinade or stock while grilling.

❖ To use leftover marinade as a sauce, bring it to a boil before serving then pour it over fish.

Belgian Endive with Walnut Vinaigrette

4 SERVINGS

2 small heads radicchio
2 heads Belgian endive
¼ cup chopped walnuts
¼ cup crumbled blue cheese
3 tablespoons minced scallions
    (green part only)

2 tablespoons rice vinegar
1 tablespoon walnut oil
½ teaspoon Dijon mustard

Separate radicchio and Belgian endive into petals. Arrange radicchio on individual plates. Place endive in daisy patterns on top of radicchio. Sprinkle with walnuts, cheese, and scallions, so that each endive petal contains a bit of each.

In a cup, whisk together vinegar, oil, and mustard. Drizzle over each salad.

Chicken Liver Pâté

6 TO 8 SERVINGS

The slightly unorthodox addition of a little potato gives this pâté a pleasant consistency and cuts down on the amount of butter required.

1 onion, minced
2 tablespoons butter or
    margarine
½ pound chicken livers
1 clove garlic, minced
1 small potato, boiled and
    chopped

1 teaspoon low-sodium soy sauce
½ teaspoon dried thyme
¼ teaspoon dried tarragon
¼ teaspoon dried sage
    pinch of cayenne pepper

Sauté onions in butter or margarine until limp. Add chicken livers and garlic and continue cooking until livers have lost their pink color. Stir in potatoes, soy sauce, thyme, tarragon, sage, and cayenne. Transfer mixture to a food processor or blender. Process until smooth. Transfer to a bowl, cover, and refrigerate overnight.

Chicken Liver Terrine in Aspic

6 SERVINGS

This makes a handsome dish decorated with fresh herbs and presented on a serving platter garnished with chopped aspic. For a simpler dish, however, you may cut aspic recipe in half, pour it over cooled terrine, chill until firm and serve directly from baking dish. Serve as an appetizer with crackers or rye bread, or serve as the first course for your picnic garnished with lettuce.

Terrine

½ pound chicken livers, trimmed
    of membranes and fat
½ pound lean ground beef
1 egg or ¼ cup egg substitute
1 clove garlic, minced
1 teaspoon dried thyme
½ teaspoon dried sage
½ teaspoon grated nutmeg
    pinch of cayenne pepper

Aspic

1 cup chicken stock
1 envelope unflavored gelatin
½ teaspoon dried tarragon
    parsley sprigs for garnish

To prepare the terrine: Preheat oven to 350°F. Mince livers with sharp knife or in food processor. Beat in beef, egg, garlic, thyme, sage, nutmeg, and cayenne. Transfer mixture to a small terrine or a 7 × 3-inch loaf pan. Bake until mixture is firm and begins to pull away from sides of pan, about 30 minutes. Remove from oven and pour off accumulated fat. Cover terrine with foil. Place weights, such as cans of food, on top of it to compress mixture. Refrigerate with weights in place overnight.

To prepare the aspic: Combine stock and gelatin in a 1-quart saucepan. Cook over medium heat, stirring, until gelatin is dissolved. Stir in tarragon and set aside to cool.

Pour half of the aspic in a small shallow pan and refrigerate until firm. Reserve to use as garnish. Place remaining aspic in refrigerator for about 10 minutes, or until it's just beginning to thicken, to use as coating for terrine.

Unmold terrine and place it on a large platter. Spoon one-third of aspic over top and sides. Refrigerate for a few minutes to set aspic. Arrange parsley sprigs on top, then coat with half of remaining aspic. Refrigerate again until firm, then cover with remaining aspic and refrigerate until completely set.

Coarsely chop reserved aspic for garnish. Distribute it around terrine.

Chicken Satay

4 SERVINGS

A *satay* is an Indonesian form of kabob. Serve with one or more of the following sauces plus rice and shredded vegetables. To use as finger food, wrap grilled meat in tender lettuce leaves.

1 pound boneless, skinless chicken breasts	½ teaspoon minced ginger root
¼ cup chicken stock	1 clove garlic, minced
1 tablespoon low-sodium soy sauce	Tahini Sauce, Cashew-Ginger Sauce, or Plum Sauce (recipes follow)
1 teaspoon honey	
½ teaspoon Szechuan peppercorns, lightly crushed	

Cut chicken into 1-inch chunks. In a shallow baking dish, combine stock, soy sauce, honey, peppercorns, ginger, and garlic. Add chicken and toss to coat. Cover and refrigerate for 1 hour.

Reserve marinade for use in Tahini Sauce. Thread chicken onto 6-inch bamboo skewers. Grill for about 3 minutes on each side, or until chicken is cooked through. Serve with Tahini Sauce, Cashew-Ginger Sauce, or Plum Sauce.

Tahini Sauce

ABOUT ½ CUP

reserved marinade from Chicken Satay	1 teaspoon lemon juice
chicken stock	⅛ teaspoon ground cumin
2 tablespoons tahini (sesame seed paste)	dash of chili oil

In a small saucepan, combine marinade and enough chicken stock to equal ¼ cup. Add tahini, lemon juice, cumin, and oil. Bring to a boil, stirring frequently. Serve immediately.

Cashew-Ginger Sauce

ABOUT ½ CUP

¼ cup skim milk
¼ cup raw cashews
¼ teaspoon minced ginger root

¼ teaspoon lime juice
pinch of ground coriander

In a food processor or blender, blend milk and cashews until smooth. Add ginger, lime juice, and coriander. Serve immediately.

Plum Sauce

ABOUT ¾ CUP

⅔ cup plum preserves or plum
    butter
4 teaspoons orange juice
2 teaspoons red wine vinegar
¼ teaspoon dry mustard

⅛ teaspoon low-sodium soy
    sauce
⅛ teaspoon grated orange peel
pinch of ground cardamom

In a small saucepan, combine preserves or butter, orange juice, vinegar, mustard, soy sauce, orange peel, and cardamom. Cook over low heat, stirring frequently, until mixture is smooth. Serve warm.

Crushed Eggplant Salad

4 TO 6 SERVINGS

Gently crushing eggplant allows it to absorb flavors readily.

3 sweet peppers, red, green, and yellow
1 large eggplant (about 1 ⅓ pounds)
1 large tomato, chopped
1 tablespoon toasted sesame seeds

2 tablespoons minced onions
1 clove garlic, minced
3 tablespoons minced fresh basil
2 tablespoons lemon juice
1 tablespoon olive oil

Roast and skin peppers and slice into strips.

Boil eggplant until tender, about 20 minutes. When cool enough to handle, peel. Chop eggplant into 1-inch cubes and crush gently with a flat spatula. Scoop crushed eggplant into a serving bowl, add remaining ingredients, and toss well.

Dilled Shrimp and Rice Salad

4 SERVINGS

Because this rice salad has its origins in Italian cuisine, it is best served on a bed of shredded radicchio and arugula greens.

3 tablespoons lemon juice
3 tablespoons olive oil
1 tablespoon red wine vinegar
1 tablespoon minced fresh dill
1 tablespoon minced fresh parsley
2 cloves garlic, minced

1 pound medium-size shrimp, cooked, peeled, and deveined
⅓ cup finely chopped red onions
4 cups cooked brown rice, cooled
1 green pepper, finely chopped
¼ cup black currants

In a large bowl, whisk together lemon juice, oil, vinegar, dill, parsley, and garlic. Add shrimp and onions and stir well to coat with dressing. Chill for 1 hour. Gently fold in rice, peppers, and currants.

Eggs Stuffed with Roquefort

6 TO 8 SERVINGS

Stuffed eggs are standard picnic fare. If you cut them in half crosswise rather than lengthwise, you can pack them into clean empty egg cartons for easy transportation.

12 hard-cooked eggs
¼ cup crumbled Roquefort
    cheese

¼ cup milk
    paprika, to sprinkle

Carefully cut eggs in half crosswise and remove yolks. Transfer yolks to a medium-size bowl. Add Roquefort and mash with a fork. Add enough milk to make a paste. Spoon into egg whites. Sprinkle with paprika.

Garden Meat Loaf

8 SERVINGS

Use a slice of cheese, a little mayonnaise, and a slice of Garden Meat Loaf for a wonderful sandwich.

¾ pound lean ground beef
1 cup cooked brown rice
1 cup whole grain bread crumbs
1 medium-size onion, chopped
2 egg whites, slightly beaten, or
    ¼ cup egg substitute
1 cup grated sweet potatoes,
    winter squash, or carrots
    (squeeze out liquid)

1½ teaspoons Worcestershire
    sauce
2 tablespoons minced fresh
    flat-leaf parsley

Preheat oven to 350°F.
In a medium-size bowl, mix together all ingredients until well-combined. Spray an 8½ × 4½-inch loaf pan with vegetable cooking spray. Add mixture, gently smoothing top, and bake for 50 to 60 minutes.

Greek Garden Kabobs

4 SERVINGS

½ cup plain-low-fat yogurt
2 tablespoons minced fresh mint
2 cloves garlic, minced
½ teaspoon dried oregano

1 large eggplant (about 1
  pound), cut into 1½-inch
  chunks
20 cherry tomatoes

In a shallow baking dish, combine yogurt, mint, garlic, and oregano. Add eggplant and toss to coat well. Cover and let marinate in the refrigerator for 30 minutes.

Thread eggplant and tomatoes onto skewers. Grill for about 2 minutes on each side. Use remaining marinade as a sauce.

Grilled Chicken with Three Mustards

4 SERVINGS

3 tablespoons apple cider
  vinegar
2 tablespoons Dijon mustard
2 tablespoons coarse mustard

½ teaspoon mustard seeds,
  crushed
1 2½-pound chicken
½ cup chicken stock

Preheat oven to 350°F.

In a small bowl, combine vinegar, Dijon mustard, coarse mustard, and mustard seeds. Spread on chicken. Cover and let marinate in the refrigerator at least 1 hour.

Bake chicken in a shallow dish for 15 to 20 minutes.

Transfer to a grill and cook for 30 to 40 minutes more, turning and basting frequently with stock.

Grilled Swordfish

4 SERVINGS

juice of 1 lemon
juice of 1 lime
½ teaspoon fennel seeds, crushed
¼ teaspoon mustard seeds, crushed

10 saffron threads, crushed
1 bay leaf
1 pound swordfish, about 1 inch thick

In a shallow baking dish that's large enough to hold fish in a single layer, combine lemon juice, lime juice, fennel seeds, mustard seeds, saffron, and bay leaf. Add fish and let marinate in the refrigerator for 30 minutes per side.

Grill fish for 5 minutes on each side.

Lentil Salad

6 TO 8 SERVINGS

2 cups lentils
8 cups water
1 bay leaf
1 teaspoon dried thyme
2 cloves garlic minced

⅓ cup olive oil
3 tablespoons vinegar
4 scallions, sliced
1 green pepper, finely chopped
¼ cup minced fresh parsley

In a medium-size saucepan, combine lentils, water, bay leaf, and thyme. Simmer for 30 minutes, or until tender. Drain. Remove bay leaf. While still warm, mix lentils with garlic, oil, and vinegar. Refrigerate until cool. Mix in scallions, peppers, and parsley.

London Broil

4 SERVINGS

2 cloves garlic, minced
1 ¼-inch slice ginger root, minced
3 allspice berries, crushed
½ teaspoon coriander seeds, crushed
¼ teaspoon mustard seeds, crushed
1 bay leaf

2 teaspoons Worcestershire sauce
1 pound top round, about 2 inches thick, trimmed of all visible fat
⅓ cup plain low-fat yogurt
prepared horseradish, to taste
Dijon mustard, to taste

In a shallow baking dish, combine garlic, ginger, allspice, coriander seeds, mustard seeds, bay leaf, and Worcestershire. Add meat and rub marinade into it on both sides. Cover and refrigerate for 5 hours or overnight.

Grill for 7 to 8 minutes per side for rare meat. Carve into thin slices and serve hot or cold.

Make a dipping sauce by combining yogurt, horseradish, and mustard.

Marinated Salmon Steaks

4 SERVINGS

This is a favorite dish when it's served with lightly steamed asparagus.

5 cardamom pods
1 allspice berry
2 cloves garlic, minced
⅓ cup lime juice

1 ⅓ pounds salmon steaks, about 1 inch thick
lime slices for garnish

Remove seeds from cardamom pods. Pulverize seeds and allspice berry with a spice mill or mortar and pestle. Combine with garlic and lime juice in a small bowl.

Arrange salmon steaks in a single layer in a shallow baking dish. Pour marinade over them and let stand for 15 minutes. Turn over and let stand 15 minutes longer.

Remove salmon from marinade. Broil or grill for 5 minutes per side, or until cooked through. Garnish with lime slices and serve.

Med Club Sandwich

4 SERVINGS

This is a good, filling dinner sandwich. The eggplant spread can be used hot or at room temperature.

2 tablespoons olive oil or other vegetable oil, divided
1 large eggplant, cut into ½-inch cubes
1 sweet red pepper, minced
1 onion, minced
3 cloves garlic, minced
¾ cup tomato sauce

2 tablespoons chopped fresh parsley
6 whole wheat pitas
½ pound cooked turkey breast, thinly sliced
4 hard-cooked eggs, thinly sliced
8 ounces provolone cheese, thinly sliced

In a large, heavy skillet, heat 1 tablespoon of the oil. Add eggplant and sauté over medium heat, stirring often, for 5 minutes, or until almost cooked through. Add remaining oil, peppers, onions, and garlic. Sauté for 1 to 2 minutes. Add tomato sauce and continue cooking over medium heat until thickened, about 5 minutes. Stir in parsley.

Cut pitas in half horizontally to make 12 slices. Roll up turkey slices and place on 4 of the pita bottoms. Top with egg slices. Place a pita slice on top of each sandwich as the middle layer. Spoon on eggplant mixture. Roll up provolone slices and place on top of eggplant. Place pita slices on top. Cut sandwiches into quarters.

Peanut Chicken

4 SERVINGS

2 whole chicken breasts, skinned, boned, and split
¼ cup peanut butter
1 small red chili pepper, seeded and minced
1 teaspoon ground cumin
1 teaspoon ground coriander
½ teaspoon cayenne pepper

3 tablespoons low-sodium soy sauce
1 tablespoon lemon juice
1 tablespoon honey
3 cloves garlic, minced
1 pound spinach, shredded and lightly steamed

Wash chicken and pat dry. Cut chicken into pieces 1 inch wide and 2½ inches long. Arrange in a single layer in a large shallow baking dish.

In a small bowl, combine peanut butter, chili peppers, cumin, coriander, cayenne, soy sauce, lemon juice, honey, and garlic. (If sauce is very thick, thin it with a little warm water.) Pour over chicken. Allow to marinate for several hours or overnight in the refrigerator, turning occasionally to coat all sides.

Remove chicken from marinade. Broil 5 inches from heat until brown, 7 to 10 minutes on each side. Baste with marinade during broiling. Serve on spinach.

Ratatouille

8 TO 10 SERVINGS

Ratatouille, which has been popular in France for generations, is an ideal picnic dish. It can be made three or four days ahead, doesn't require last-minute chilling, and is extremely flexible as far as ingredients go. The rule of thumb is to use approximately equal amounts of vegetables, but you can vary the recipes to suit yourself.

2 onions, minced
1 tablespoon olive oil
1 tablespoon dried thyme
1 teaspoon dried basil
½ teaspoon dried rosemary
3 cloves garlic, minced
   pinch of red pepper flakes, or
      to taste

1 eggplant, diced
6 zucchini, sliced
2 sweet red peppers, chopped
4 to 6 tomatoes, peeled, seeded,
      and chopped

In a Dutch oven, sauté onions in oil over medium-low heat until they have started to soften. Add thyme, basil, rosemary, garlic, and red pepper flakes. Continue cooking until onions are translucent. Add eggplant, zucchini, and peppers. Cook about 5 minutes, stirring occasionally. Add tomatoes and continue cooking until vegetables are tender. Chill overnight.

Salade Nicoise

6 TO 8 SERVINGS

This is a satisfying salad to have on a picnic since it can be assembled on the spot. Take along washed lettuce and a knife for cutting potatoes, eggs, and tomatoes. Even without traditional anchovies and olives, this salad is delectable.

¼ cup olive oil	1 cup cooked green beans
2 tablespoons vinegar	4 potatoes, boiled
1 teaspoon Dijon mustard	4 tomatoes
1 head Boston or romaine lettuce	4 hard-cooked eggs
1 6½ or 7-ounce can tuna, drained and flaked	

Combine oil, vinegar, and mustard in a jar with a tight-fitting lid. Shake well just before using.

Just before serving, tear lettuce into bite-size pieces, and combine in a large bowl with tuna and beans. Slice potatoes and quarter tomatoes and eggs. Add to the bowl. Drizzle with enough dressing to lightly coat.

Petite Pâté Sandwiches

4 TO 6 SERVINGS

1 pound chicken livers	1 teaspoon prepared mustard
1 onion, chopped	dash of hot pepper sauce
1 tablespoon butter or margarine	4 to 6 croissants or crescent rolls
pinch of dried sage	½ to ¾ cup coarsely chopped pimiento
pinch of dried thyme	
pinch of dried rosemary	½ to ¾ cup fresh parsley clusters

Sauté livers and onions in butter or margarine for 1 to 2 minutes. Add sage, thyme, rosemary, mustard, and hot pepper sauce and sauté until livers are cooked, about 10 minutes. Puree in a food processor or blender and then chill.

Slice croissants in half horizontally. Spread bottoms with pâté. Top with pimiento and parsley. Replace tops.

Sea Kabobs Salad with Curry Vinaigrette

4 SERVINGS

Salad

¼ cup rice vinegar
3 bay leaves
2 cloves garlic, minced
1 teaspoon green peppercorns, crushed*
⅓ pound jumbo shrimp, peeled and deveined
⅓ pound large sea scallops
⅓ pound shark, cut into 1-inch chunks
3 sweet peppers, red, green, and yellow

Vinaigrette

2 tablespoons rice vinegar
½ teaspoon Dijon mustard
½ teaspoon coarse mustard
½ teaspoon green peppercorns, crushed
½ teaspoon curry powder
1 clove garlic, minced
freshly ground black pepper

To prepare the salad: In a shallow baking dish, combine vinegar, bay leaves, garlic, and peppercorns. Add shrimp, scallops, and shark. Toss to coat. Cover and allow to marinate in the refrigerator for 1 hour.

Meanwhile, cut peppers in half and remove seeds. Grill, skin side toward heat source, for 8 to 10 minutes. If desired, remove skin. Cut peppers into very thin slices and transfer to a large bowl.

Thread shrimp, scallops, and shark onto skewers Grill for 3 minutes on each side. When cool enough to handle, remove from skewers and add to bowl with peppers.

To prepare the vinaigrette: In a small bowl, whisk together vinegar, Dijon mustard, coarse mustard, peppercorns, curry powder, garlic, and pepper. Pour over seafood mixture. Toss to coat well. Serve immediately.

*Green peppercorns come in varying strengths. The ones used here are soft and come packed in vinegar. They are milder than both freeze-dried peppercorns and sun-dried ones (which are the hottest). If using the more fiery varieties, reduce quantities accordingly.

Simple Salmon Sandwiches

4 SERVINGS

1 tablespoon mayonnaise	8 slices whole wheat toast
¼ cup plain low-fat yogurt	8 scallions
2 tablespoons chopped fresh dill	8 thin slices Swiss cheese
1 15½-ounce can salmon, drained and flaked	

Combine mayonnaise, yogurt, and dill in a small bowl. Mix salmon with half of the dressing in a medium-size bowl. Spread salmon salad on 4 of the slices of toast. Place 2 scallions on top of each sandwich. Roll up slices of Swiss cheese and place 2 on each sandwich. Spread remaining slices of bread with remaining dressing and place on top.

Spinach Terrine

4 TO 6 SERVINGS

1 cup minced cooked spinach
1 slice whole wheat bread, crust
  removed
⅓ cup milk or chicken stock
1 onion, minced
2 cloves garlic, minced
1 teaspoon olive oil

2 eggs or ½ cup egg substitute
2 teaspoons low-sodium soy
  sauce
1 teaspoon dried thyme
1 teaspoon dried dill
2 cups cooked navy beans
6 pecan halves for garnish

Preheat oven to 350°F.

Drain spinach thoroughly in a colander and squeeze out any remaining liquid. Place in a medium-size mixing bowl.

Soak bread in milk or stock for about 5 minutes. Add to spinach.

In a nonstick skillet, cook onions and garlic in oil over medium-low heat until soft. Add to spinach, along with eggs, soy sauce, thyme, and dill. Mix well, or combine in a food processor. Stir in beans.

Coat a medium-size terrine or an 8½ × 4½-inch loaf pan with vegetable cooking spray. Pour in spinach mixture. Bake until mixture is set and begins to pull away from sides of pan, about 30 minutes.

To serve warm, let stand at room temperature 5 to 10 minutes to set. To serve cold, refrigerate for several hours or overnight. Unmold and decorate top with line of pecans.

Stuffed Swiss Chard

4 SERVINGS

12 to 15 large Swiss chard leaves
1 teaspoon vegetable oil
1 medium-size onion, finely
   chopped
½ cup cooked brown rice
½ cup cooked ground meat
¼ cup grated Swiss cheese
½ teaspoon freshly grated
   nutmeg

⅛ teaspoon freshly ground white
   pepper, or to taste
2 cups finely chopped peeled
   cooking apples
¼ cup apple juice
¼ cup chicken stock
2 bay leaves
3 peppercorns

Preheat oven to 350°F.

With a paring knife, shave off excess rib from center of each chard leaf down to the stem. Cut off stems. Steam chard leaves for about 40 seconds, or until bright green and flexible enough to roll. Drain, then pat dry with paper towels.

Heat oil in a nonstick skillet and add onions. Cook until soft, about 5 minutes. Remove from heat and stir in rice, meat, cheese, nutmeg, pepper, and apples.

Place 2 tablespoons of filling on center of each leaf. Fold up stem ends, then fold sides over filling. Roll up leaf to form a packet and place into a 9 × 13-inch baking dish.

Combine juice, stock, bay leaves, and peppercorns. Pour over chard leaves. Cover tightly with foil. Bake until leaves are tender and filling is heated through, about 20 to 25 minutes. Baste 2 or 3 times while baking. Before serving, remove bay leaves and spoon pan juices over each serving.

West Texas Barbecue Sauce

2½ CUPS

Use this sauce on ribs or chicken for the last 3 to 5 minutes of grilling. You can also serve it as a dipping sauce at the table or toss with leftover meats and poultry to make sandwich fillings. If you intend to freeze sauce, leave out ground pepper and cayenne; add them just before serving.

1½ tablespoons butter or margarine	⅔ cup apple cider vinegar
2 celery stalks, minced	½ cup apple juice
3 scallions, minced	¼ cup Worcestershire sauce
2 cloves garlic, minced	1½ teaspoons honey
2 bay leaves	15 peppercorns, ground
1½ cups tomato puree	dash of cayenne pepper

In a large saucepan, melt butter or margarine. Add celery, scallions, garlic, and bay leaves. Sauté for 5 minutes. Add tomato puree, vinegar, juice, Worcestershire, and honey. Bring to a boil. Reduce heat and simmer, uncovered, for 35 minutes. Add pepper and cayenne and simmer 5 minutes more. Remove bay leaves before serving.

Yakitori

4 SERVINGS

1¼ pounds sea scallops
8 scallions, thinly sliced
¼ cup low-sodium soy sauce
3 tablespoons *mirin** (sweet rice vinegar)
3 tablespoons water

juice of one-half lemon
1½ tablespoons minced ginger root
1 tablespoon grated orange peel
4 tablespoons *wasabi** (Japanese horseradish)

Wash scallops to remove any sand. Pat dry and set aside.

In a large shallow bowl, combine scallions, soy sauce, *mirin*, water, lemon juice, ginger, and orange peel. Add scallops. Toss to coat well. Cover and allow to marinate for 1 to 2 hours.

Soak 15 bamboo skewers in water for an hour. Remove scallops from marinade and place on skewers. Grill or broil close to heat. Brush with marinade during cooking and turn skewers until scallops are quite brown on both sides.

In a small bowl, mix the *wasabi* with enough water to form a thick paste. Serve with scallops as a dipping sauce.

*Available in Oriental markets.

Zesty Pesto Hero

4 SERVINGS

Pesto is not just for pasta or potatoes. As a sandwich spread, it blends beautifully with any salad vegetable from arugula to zucchini, stacked as high as you please!

2 cloves garlic	2 loaves whole wheat French
1½ cups loosely packed fresh	bread
basil	2 tomatoes, thinly sliced
½ cup pine nuts	1 red onion, thinly sliced
¾ cup grated Parmesan cheese	12 mushrooms, thinly sliced
3 to 5 tablespoons olive oil	

In a food processor, mince garlic. Add basil and pine nuts and process until minced. Add cheese and process until well blended. With motor running, slowly pour in oil, adding only enough to make a thick spread. Continue processing until well-blended.

Cut loaves of bread in half crosswise, then slice each piece in half horizontally. Spread cut side of each piece with pesto. On the 4 bottom pieces, place a layer of tomatoes, then onions, then mushrooms. Place remaining pieces of bread on top.

Beautiful Breads

Everyone loves the aroma of freshly baked bread! Whether you're baking yeast breads or quick breads, you can experiment with whole-grain combinations that will add flavor as well as nutrients. Try small amounts of rye, cornmeal, or buckwheat mixed with wheat flour, for example. Rye yields a moist, dense loaf; cornmeal adds a slightly dry, grainy texture, while a little buckwheat flour gives whole wheat bread a pleasing, old-world taste. The opportunities for tasty discovery are almost endless. But keep the pairings fairly simple so the flavor of each flour retains its own identity.

Through experimenting we have found that the following combinations of nonwheat flours and ground grains complement each other in nutritional value and the final texture of the bread in which they're used:

❖ Rye flour plus barley flour
❖ Brown rice flour plus ground millet
❖ Cornmeal plus brown rice flour
❖ Gluten flour plus soy flour
❖ Triticale flour plus cornmeal

You may substitute them for up to one-quarter of the amount of whole wheat flour called for in a recipe. If you use more than that in a yeast bread, your loaf won't rise well. Only wheat flour contains the proper gluten-forming protein needed to take advantage of yeast's rising action. Rye and triticale flours contain only small amounts of gluten—too little to provide a good rise on their own.

Yeast Breads

Yeast breads are the ultimate in bread baking and eating. But many cooks are afraid to try them. Be brave and try at least one of the recipes here. You'll soon see how easy it is to take the mystery out of making yeast breads.

How to Bake a Salt-Free Bread

1. When you eliminate salt in a yeast bread, the rising time will be cut, sometimes by as much as half. Just let the dough rise until nearly doubled in bulk, paying no attention to the rising time in the recipe.

2. Since less liquid will be absorbed when you omit salt from the recipe, the dough may seem too damp after the first rise. Compensate by adding more flour and thoroughly kneading it into the dough.

3. Don't worry about rising time and moisture in quick breads that use baking powder and/or baking soda. Eliminating the salt will affect only the taste.

Quick Breads

Living up to their name, quick breads can be made in much less time than yeast breads. Sweetened, spiced, herbed, or filled, these breads offer as many delicious variations as yeast breads. You can vary them in numerous ways. A cupful of chopped nuts adds new appeal to a plain banana bread. A pureed vegetable imparts its own flavor when it replaces some of the liquid in a recipe.

We find homemade bread makes even a mundane meal special. And these recipes are for the best of home-made breads!

Dilled Carrot Bread

1 LARGE LOAF

1 tablespoon dry yeast
¼ cup warm water (105° to 115°F)
2 teaspoons honey
1¼ cups shredded carrots
¾ cup creamed cottage cheese, heated to lukewarm
1 egg, slightly beaten
¼ cup grated Parmesan cheese
1 tablespoon butter, softened

1 tablespoon minced fresh dill
1 teaspoon dill seeds
½ teaspoon caraway seeds, optional
½ teaspoon salt
1¾ cups whole wheat flour
1 to 1¼ cups unbleached white flour
1 egg, beaten with 1 teaspoon milk

Sprinkle yeast over warm water and honey in a large warm bowl. Cover with a towel and let rest 10 minutes. Stir. Add carrots, cottage cheese, 1 beaten egg, Parmesan cheese, butter, minced dill, dill seeds, caraway seeds, and salt. Stir in whole wheat flour and unbleached white flour, 1 cup at a time, using a wooden spoon. Add enough flour so that dough comes away from the sides of the bowl but remains sticky. Place in a bowl that has been coated with vegetable cooking spray. Cover bowl with plastic wrap and towels, place in a warm spot, and let rise until doubled in bulk, about 1 hour.

Stir dough down with an oiled spoon. Turn into an oiled 9 ×5-inch loaf pan or a 1½-quart casserole dish. Flour your hands lightly and pat in dough evenly. Cover with a towel. Let rise in a warm place until doubled in bulk, about 45 minutes.

Brush with egg mixture and bake in a preheated 375°F oven for 40 to 45 minutes, or until bread tests done. Cool in pan 10 minutes.

Remove from pan and cool on wire rack.

Parmesan Bread

1 LOAF

1 package dry yeast
¼ cup warm water
¼ cup milk, scalded and cooled
  to room temperature
1½ cups whole wheat flour
½ teaspoon salt
5 tablespoons unsalted butter

1 egg, beaten
½ cup grated Parmesan cheese
2 tablespoons chopped fresh
  parsley
2 tablespoons chopped
  scallions
1 teaspoon honey

Dissolve yeast in lukewarm water. Scald milk and let it cool. Then combine yeast mixture with milk. Set aside.

Combine flour and salt. Cut in butter with a pastry blender or 2 knives until mixture resembles coarse crumbs. Fold in yeast mixture and then add beaten egg, cheese, parsley, scallions, and honey. Mix well.

Turn out dough onto a lightly floured surface and knead gently for 5 to 8 minutes. Place into an oiled layer cake pan. Lightly oil top of batter, cover, and let rise in a warm place for about 30 minutes.

Bake at 375°F for about 25 minutes.

Cut into wedges and serve hot.

Seven-Grain Bread

2 LOAVES

This dough takes only 15 minutes to prepare. Make the batter, and knead it just before you go to bed or first thing in the morning. Refrigerate it for at least 6 hours. (The yeast will raise the dough even without heat.) Then when you want a fresh loaf, put it in the oven to bake.

1½ cups boiling water	⅓ cup molasses
1 cup 7-grain cereal	3 tablespoons corn oil
2 packages dry yeast	3 tablespoons butter
¼ cup warm water (105° to 115°F)	3 eggs, beaten
¼ cup buttermilk	4½ to 5 cups whole wheat flour

In a large mixing bowl, pour boiling water over 7-grain cereal. Let cool to room temperature.

In a small bowl, dissolve yeast in warm water. Set aside until foamy, about 10 minutes. Stir in honey and set aside.

In a small saucepan, combine buttermilk, molasses, oil, and butter. Heat mixture until lukewarm.

Add buttermilk mixture, yeast, and eggs to cereal. Mix well with a wooden spoon. Stir in about 4 cups of the flour, a little at a time. The mixture will be crumbly but damp.

Turn out dough onto a lightly floured surface and knead in the remaining flour until dough is smooth but slightly damp (about 8 to 10 minutes). Divide dough in half and place each portion into an 8 × 4-inch loaf pan that has been well coated with vegetable cooking spray. Cover each pan with waxed paper and place in refrigerator for at least 6 hours.

Remove pans from refrigerator, uncover, and immediately place in cold oven. Set oven temperature to 375°F and bake for 50 minutes, or until loaves sound hollow when tapped.

Remove from pans and cool on wire racks.

Apple Caraway Bread

1 LOAF

2 cups whole wheat flour
1 teaspoon baking powder
½ teaspoon baking soda
½ cup butter
¼ cup honey
¼ cup shredded sharp cheddar
  cheese

1 cup unsweetened
  applesauce
2 eggs
½ cup chopped walnuts
1½ teaspoons caraway seeds

Preheat oven to 350°F.

In a large bowl, stir together flour, baking powder, and baking soda.

In a medium-size saucepan, heat butter and honey together, stirring occasionally until butter is melted. Remove from heat. Stir in cheese until it melts. Mix in applesauce, then beat in eggs, one at a time. Add walnuts and caraway seeds.

Stir the cheese mixture into dry ingredients just until combined. Transfer batter to a lightly oiled 8½ × 4½-inch loaf pan. Bake until golden brown, about 1 hour.

Remove from pan and cool on wire rack.

> VARIATIONS: You can use raw applesauce if you wish. Just blend chopped apples with a little apple juice until smooth.
>
> You can also substitute ½ cup sunflower oil for the butter. Heat with the honey, then proceed as directed.

Chili Con Queso Corn Bread

8 TO 10 SERVINGS

¼ cup vegetable oil, divided
½ cup chopped onions
½ sweet red pepper, finely
    chopped
1 cup yellow cornmeal
½ cup whole wheat flour
1 tablespoon baking powder
½ teaspoon baking soda
½ teaspoon dried oregano

1 cup cooked corn kernels
½ cup heavy cream
2 eggs
1 cup buttermilk
1½ cups shredded sharp
    cheddar cheese, divided
4 jalapeño peppers, roasted,
    peeled, seeded, and
    chopped

Preheat oven to 400°F.

Heat 1 tablespoon of the oil in a 10-inch cast-iron skillet or porcelain-coated iron skillet with a heat-proof or removable handle. Sauté onions and red peppers for 5 minutes, then remove them to a small plate to cool.

Add one teaspoon of the oil to skillet and keep it hot.

Combine cornmeal, flour, baking powder, baking soda, and oregano in a large bowl.

Blend two-thirds of the corn with cream in a blender on medium speed for 5 seconds, or until kernels are coarsely chopped. Add eggs, buttermilk, and remaining oil and blend again. Pour over dry ingredients. Stir in remaining corn, onion mixture, 1 cup of the shredded cheese, and jalapeño peppers. Pour mixture into hot skillet and sprinkle top with remaining cheese. Bake 30 to 35 minutes, or until golden brown.

Cool in skillet on wire rack for 15 to 20 minutes. Cut into wedges and serve warm.

Currant Buttermilk Biscuit

2 SERVINGS

This is a quick, no-fuss bread.

½ cup whole wheat flour
½ cup unbleached white flour
½ teaspoon baking soda
½ teaspoon baking powder
¼ teaspoon ground cinnamon

¼ cup cold butter, cut into pieces
2 tablespoons currants
¼ cup buttermilk
1 tablespoon honey

Preheat oven to 350°F. Lightly oil an 8-inch layer cake pan.

Combine whole wheat flour, unbleached white flour, baking soda, baking powder, and cinnamon in a medium-size bowl or a food processor. Cut butter into flour, using 2 knives, a pastry blender, or several on-off turns of the processor. When the dry ingredients resemble coarse meal, stir in currants, buttermilk, and honey. Form dough into a large ball and place into prepared pan. Bake for 15 minutes. Then, using a sharp paring knife, cut an "X" in the top of the biscuit about 1 inch deep. Continue to bake until golden brown, 25 to 30 minutes.

Remove from pan and cool on wire rack.

VARIATION: Add ¼ teaspoon grated orange peel to the dry ingredients. Substitute 2 tablespoons finely chopped raisins for the currants.

Onion Dill Bread

2 LOAVES

1 cup finely chopped onions	2 tablespoons baking powder
⅓ cup minced fresh dill or 2 tablespoons dried dill	1 tablespoon honey
7 to 8 cups whole wheat flour	4 cups buttermilk
½ teaspoon baking soda	celery seeds for garnish
	dill seeds for garnish

Preheat oven to 350°F.

In a nonstick medium-size skillet coated with vegetable cooking spray, sauté onions until translucent. Add dill and continue to sauté until wilted. Set aside.

In a large bowl, combine 7 cups of the flour, baking soda, and baking powder. Add onion mixture and combine well. Add honey and continue mixing as you add buttermilk. If dough is too sticky, add more flour. Blend thoroughly and when dough is smooth, divide it in half.

Form dough into rounds, ovals, or rectangles and set on a lightly oiled and floured baking sheet. With a sharp knife, slash a deep cross into each loaf. Spray them with just enough water to moisten and gently press in seeds. Bake until crust is dark brown, 40 to 50 minutes.

Remove from baking sheet and cool on wire racks.

Orange Spice Bread

1 LOAF

½ cup butter, melted
½ cup honey
½ cup orange juice
½ cup skim milk
2 eggs
1½ teaspoons grated orange peel

¼ teaspoon almond extract
2 cups whole wheat pastry flour
⅓ cup unbleached white flour
2 teaspoons baking powder
¼ teaspoon ground allspice
¼ teaspoon ground cardamom
⅛ teaspoon grated nutmeg

Preheat oven to 350°F.

In a large bowl, combine butter, honey, and orange juice. Stir in milk, then beat in eggs until well combined. Add orange peel and almond extract.

In a medium-size bowl, combine whole wheat pastry flour, unbleached white flour, baking powder, and spices. Stir dry ingredients into orange juice mixture just until blended. Pour batter into a lightly oiled 8½ × 4½-inch loaf pan. Bake until a cake tester inserted into center comes out clean, 55 to 60 minutes.

Remove from pan and cool on a wire rack.

VARIATION: Add 1 cup coarsely chopped pecans to dry ingredients before adding them to orange juice mixture.

Sally Lunn

2 RECTANGULAR LOAVES OR 1 ROUND LOAF

½ cup plus 1 teaspoon honey,
   divided
¼ cup warm water
2 teaspoons dry yeast
1¾ cups milk, scalded
1 cup dried currants, optional
½ cup butter, melted

2 teaspoons ground cinnamon
1 cup chopped walnuts,
   optional
3 cups whole wheat flour, at
   room temperature
3 eggs, at room temperature,
   separated

Combine 1 teaspoon of the honey and warm water in a
small bowl. Dissolve yeast in mixture and set aside to proof.
Mix together milk, currants, and butter. Mix in cinnamon and
walnuts, if using, with flour.

Using an electric mixer, beat egg yolks briefly in a large
bowl. Add ½ of the honey and beat until fluffy. Beat in yeast and
milk mixtures. Gradually add flour mixture, and beat hard for
3 minutes.

Beat egg whites until stiff. Fold one-quarter of them
thoroughly into batter. Then gently fold in remaining
egg whites.

Generously butter two 9 × 5-inch pans or one 9-inch
tube pan.

Gently turn batter into prepared pans. Set pans into a
large pan of warm water and let rise in a warm place for about
1 hour.

Carefully lift pans out of water and into cold oven. Set
oven to 400°F. Bake for 15 minutes. Reduce heat to 325°F and
continue to bake for 25 to 30 minutes, or until a cake tester
inserted into center comes out clean.

Remove pans from oven and cool for 5 minutes on a wire
rack. Gently loosen bread from sides of pans and carefully turn
out bread. Cool completely on wire rack.

Orange Muffins

12 MUFFINS

This recipe uses orange juice instead of milk for a lovely orange taste.

1½ cups whole wheat flour	grated peel of 1 orange
½ cup bran or 100% bran cereal	¼ cup honey
1½ teaspoons baking soda	2 tablespoons vegetable oil or
¾ cup orange juice	melted butter
1 egg, beaten	½ cup raisins

Preheat oven to 375°F. Butter a 12-cup muffin tin or line it with paper liners.

In a large mixing bowl, combine flour, bran or bran cereal, and baking soda.

In a separate bowl, mix together orange juice, beaten egg, orange peel, honey, oil or butter, and raisins. Combine with dry ingredients. Fill muffin cups about three-quarters full with batter and bake for 15 minutes, or until cake tester inserted into center comes out clean.

Remove from tin and cool on wire racks.

Carrot Muffins

12 MUFFINS

2 cups whole wheat flour
⅔ cup bran flakes
2 teaspoons baking powder
   pinch of ground nutmeg
1 teaspoon ground cinnamon
1 egg, beaten

1½ cups milk
2 tablespoons vegetable oil
2 tablespoons molasses
¼ cup honey
1½ cups shredded carrots
½ cup raisins

Preheat oven to 375°F. Butter a 12-cup muffin tin or line it with paper liners.

In a large mixing bowl, stir flour, bran flakes, baking powder, nutmeg, and cinnamon together.

In a medium-size bowl combine beaten egg, milk, oil, molasses, honey, carrots, and raisins. Let stand for 5 minutes, then add to flour mixture, stirring just until mixed thoroughly. Fill muffin cups about three-quarters full with batter and bake for 20 to 25 minutes.

Remove from tin and cool on wire racks.

Cornmeal Muffins

12 MUFFINS

Add some finely diced jalapeño peppers or scallions to the batter, if
you like.

½ cup whole wheat flour
2½ teaspoons baking powder
1½ cups cornmeal
2 tablespoons butter or
   margarine, melted
2 tablespoons honey

1 egg
¾ cup milk
¾ cup shredded cheddar or
   Monterey Jack cheese
1 cup cooked corn kernels

Preheat oven to 375°F. Generously butter a 12-cup
muffin tin.

Stir the flour, baking powder, and cornmeal together in a
large mixing bowl.

In another bowl, whisk the melted butter or margarine,
honey, egg, and milk together. Mix in cheese and corn. Stir into
the flour mixture just until combined. Fill muffin cups about
three-quarters full with batter and bake for 15 minutes, or until
a cake tester inserted into center comes out clean.

Remove from tin and cool on wire racks.

Maple-Nut Muffins

6 MUFFINS

This is a good recipe for two people, but it can be doubled, if you wish.

1 cup whole wheat flour	2 tablespoons vegetable oil
⅓ cup coarsely chopped pecans or walnuts	⅓ cup milk
	⅓ cup maple syrup
1 teaspoon baking powder	6 pecan halves for garnish
1 egg, beaten	

Preheat oven to 375°F. Butter or oil a 6-cup muffin tin.

Combine flour, pecans or walnuts, and baking powder in a medium-size mixing bowl.

In another medium-size bowl, mix together beaten egg, oil, milk, and syrup. Add to flour mixture, stirring just until combined. Fill muffin cups about three-quarters full with batter. Top each with a pecan half and bake for 15 to 20 minutes, or until cake tester inserted into center comes out clean.

Remove from tin and cool on wire racks.

Oatmeal-Yeast Muffins

12 MUFFINS

Yeast muffins have a bread-like quality with springy texture and well-developed crust. These are exceptionally good served with a meal in place of dinner rolls or bread.

2 teaspoons yeast	2 cups whole wheat flour
1¼ cups warm water	1 cup rolled oats
2 tablespoons vegetable oil	2 tablespoons rolled oats for
2 tablespoons honey	garnish

Blend all ingredients, except 2 tablespoons rolled oats, and beat vigorously (this may be done in a food processor with the plastic blade). Pour into a lightly oiled bowl, cover with a towel, and let rise for about 1 hour, or until doubled in bulk.

Preheat oven to 375°F. Generously butter a 12-cup muffin tin.

Punch down the dough and fill muffin cups about two-thirds full with dough. Sprinkle tops with rolled oats. Cover loosely and let rise for 15 minutes.

Bake for 20 to 30 minutes, or until a cake tester inserted into center comes out clean.

Remove from tin and cool on wire racks.

Overnight Muffins

15 MUFFINS

If you like freshly baked muffins for breakfast but don't have time to make them in the morning, try this recipe. The batter can be made ahead of time and stored in the refrigerator for several days, so it's easy to bake fresh muffins each morning.

1 cup coarsely chopped mixed dried fruit, such as apricots, dates, prunes, or raisins	1/3 cup honey
	1 egg, beaten
	1 cup buttermilk
2 teaspoons baking soda	2½ cups whole wheat flour
½ cup boiling water	
2 tablespoons butter or margarine, melted	

Preheat oven to 400°F. Butter 15 muffin cups or line with paper liners.

Combine fruit and baking soda in a large mixing bowl and pour water over mixture. Stir and let cool.

In a medium-size bowl, mix together butter or margarine and honey. Add beaten egg and then buttermilk. Add to fruit mixture along with flour, stirring just until combined. Place in an airtight container and refrigerate for several hours or overnight.

When ready to bake, fill muffin cups about three-quarters full with batter and bake for 15 minutes.

Remove from tins and cool on wire racks.

Delicious
Desserts

Do people who want to eat healthfully have to forgo desserts? No! At Rodale we make great desserts, and we do it using nutritionally rich, flavorful ingredients in exciting, mouth-watering recipes.

Wonderful Wholesome Ingredients

Since white flour is a nutritional loss, we use mostly whole grain flours in our desserts. Whole wheat pastry flour is usually the flour we select. Whole wheat does make a cake heavier than one that's made with white flour. For this reason we sometimes use up to one-half white flour to lighten a cake. It makes a big difference in texture.

We use fresh dairy products in most of our desserts, but we also use nonfat dry milk. It's low in calories and adds body that would be classically achieved with powdered sugar, which we never use.

Vegetable oil is better for you than solid shortening so we try to use it in our desserts. When a solid shortening is essential to the finished product, the only ones we use are unsalted butter or margarine.

Where we depart the most from conventional dessert recipes is in our use of sweeteners. We never use sugar, and we don't miss it at all. Honey, which is about twice as sweet as sugar, is usually our choice. While we realize that it's not exactly a nutritional blockbuster, you need only about half as much of it as you do sugar and, unlike sugar, it does contain some minerals. Look for honey that's labeled "pure honey." Without this identification honey may contain sugar or corn syrup. Since desserts are delicate, we use honeys that don't have strong, overpowering flavors, such as clover honey, orange blossom honey, or wildflower honey. Most wild honeys are light in color.

You'll find that the baked goods you make with honey keep longer than those made with sugar. Honey is a natural preservative.

Maple syrup isn't as sweet as honey (use it measure for measure when substituting for sugar), but it imparts a lovely maple flavor that won't be easily overpowered.

We use molasses in tandem with honey (1 or 2 tablespoons per cup of honey) to achieve the tang that brown sugar provides.

In many of our desserts, fresh fruit supplies all the sweetener that's needed. Nothing is lovelier or better for you than a dessert sweetened this way.

Cookie Tips

Are you a cookie lover? Here are a few tips from the Food Center that will help make the job easier and the finished product even better than ever.

❖ Save time and cleanup by rolling and cutting dough directly on the baking sheets.

❖ Use a light dusting of cornstarch, rather than flour, on the rolling surface. It works better than flour, leaves no starchy aftertaste, and quickens cleanup.

❖ As a healthful alternative to confectioners' sugar, grind puffed rice, popcorn, or coconut and sprinkle on cookies.

❖ Freshen stale cookies by heating them in the oven for about 5 minutes at 325°F.

Apple Tart

10 SERVINGS

3 to 4 medium-size baking
    apples, peeled and cut into
    ¼-inch slices
1 egg
2 egg whites
½ cup plain low-fat yogurt

¼ cup honey
¼ cup whole wheat flour
¼ teaspoon vanilla extract
1 tablespoon apple jelly
2 tablespoons apple juice

Preheat oven to 375°F.

Coat a 9-inch tart pan with removable bottom with vegetable cooking spray.

Arrange apple slices in 2 concentric circles, slightly overlapping each other in pan.

In a medium-size bowl, combine egg, egg whites, yogurt, honey, flour, and vanilla. Spoon over apple slices so that all are covered but their shapes are still visible. Bake for 30 minutes.

In a small saucepan, combine jelly and juice over low heat. Brush evenly over tart and bake 10 minutes more, or until toasty brown.

Apple Terrine

6 SERVINGS

Serve this dessert warm or cold, plain or topped with yogurt.

4 cups shredded apples
1½ cups whole grain bread
    crumbs
2 eggs or ½ cup egg substitute

½ cup skim milk
¼ cup honey
½ teaspoon vanilla extract

Preheat oven to 350°F.

Combine apples, bread crumbs, eggs, milk, honey, and vanilla in a large bowl.

Coat a medium-size terrine or an 8½ × 4½-inch loaf pan with vegetable cooking spray. Pour apple mixture into pan and bake until fairly firm to the touch and lightly browned along edges, about 45 minutes.

Frozen Apricot Mousse

8 SERVINGS

1 pound dried apricots
2 cups hot orange spice tea
1 teaspoon ground ginger

1 tablespoon unflavored gelatin
½ cup orange juice
    lime slices for decoration

Place apricots in a glass bowl. Pour hot tea over apricots and soak for 1 hour, covered.

Add ginger and puree in a food processor or blender until smooth.

In a small saucepan, stir gelatin into orange juice, then bring to a boil, stirring constantly, until dissolved. Remove from heat and add apricot mixture, blending thoroughly. Pour into individual molds (or 1 5-cup mold) and freeze for about 4 hours.

To serve, unmold and garnish with lime slices.

Fragrant Pear Charlotte

8 TO 10 SERVINGS

3 pounds pears, peeled, cored,
and chopped
¼ teaspoon grated orange peel
1 vanilla bean
12 slices whole grain bread,
crusts removed
½ cup raspberry or apricot
preserves

¼ cup apple juice
plain low-fat yogurt, flavored
with vanilla and sweetened
with honey to taste, for
topping
fresh or sautéed pear slices
for garnish

In a medium-size skillet, combine pears, orange peel, and vanilla bean. Simmer, stirring frequently, for about 30 minutes, or until pears are very thick. Drain off any excess liquid. Remove and discard vanilla bean.

Cut 5 slices of bread in half diagonally. Fit them into the bottom of an 8½-inch round, glass baking dish, trimming slices as necessary to cover bottom. Cut remaining slices into 1-inch strips and fit them around the sides of dish to completely cover. Carefully remove all slices from dish and set aside.

Preheat oven to 450°F. Spray baking dish with vegetable cooking spray.

In a small bowl, combine the preserves and juice. If preserves are too thick, heat briefly to liquefy. Dip both sides of each piece of bread in the mixture and refit into the baking dish. Spoon pear mixture into dish and bake for 15 minutes. Reduce oven temperature to 350°F and bake for another 30 minutes. Let cool in dish. Cover and refrigerate overnight.

To serve, run the blade of a knife around edge of dish to loosen bread. Place a serving platter on top of dish and invert to unmold charlotte. Serve with yogurt and pear slices.

Classic Carrot Cake

20 SERVINGS

Cake

1½ cups whole wheat pastry flour
1½ cups unbleached white flour
2 teaspoons baking powder
½ teaspoon baking soda
1½ teaspoons ground cinnamon
¼ teaspoon ground mace
¼ teaspoon ground allspice
3 eggs
1 cup honey, warmed
1 cup corn oil
2 cups finely grated carrots,
  tightly packed
1 cup raisins, plumped in warm
  water, drained well,
  chopped, tossed with 2
  teaspoons flour
½ cup chopped pecans
1 teaspoon vanilla extract

Frosting

8 ounces cream cheese, softened
⅓ cup honey
1 teaspoon vanilla

Candied Carrot Strips

1 small carrot
¼ cup honey
½ cup water

2 tablespoons chopped pecans
  for decoration

To prepare the cake: Sift together whole wheat pastry flour, unbleached white flour, baking powder, baking soda, cinnamon, mace, and allspice into a large bowl. Set aside.

In a large bowl, beat eggs. Gradually add honey and oil and beat until well-blended. Stir in carrots, raisins, pecans, and vanilla. Stir in flour mixture, about 1 cup at a time, blending well after each addition. Pour into a 13 × 9-inch pan that has been sprayed with vegetable cooking spray. Bake at 350°F for 40 to 50 minutes, or until cake tests done. Remove to a wire rack and cool completely.

To prepare the frosting: In a medium-size bowl, cream together all ingredients until smooth, about 5 minutes.

To prepare the candied carrot strips: Using a vegetable peeler, cut thin strips, ⅛ inch thick and ½ to 1 inch long, from carrot.

Combine honey and water in a small heavy saucepan. Bring to a boil over medium heat, stirring constantly. Add carrot strips and cook until carrots are well-glazed, 15 to 20 minutes. Remove carrots with a fork to a piece of waxed paper and let cool. Frost cake, sprinkle with chopped pecans, and arrange carrot strips on top of frosting.

Crustless German Cheesecake

16 SERVINGS

2 tablespoons toasted wheat germ	⅓ cup honey
½ teaspoon ground cinnamon	⅓ cup cornstarch
1½ pounds low-fat cottage cheese	2 tablespoons lemon juice
4 eggs, separated	2 teaspoons vanilla extract
	grated peel of ½ lemon

Preheat oven to 250°F. Coat a 9-inch springform pan with vegetable cooking spray.

In a cup, mix together wheat germ and cinnamon. Add to pan, and swirl it to coat bottom and sides evenly.

In a food processor, blend cottage cheese until smooth. Add egg yolks, honey, cornstarch, lemon juice, vanilla, and lemon peel. Process to mix well. Pour into a large bowl.

In another large bowl, beat egg whites with clean beaters until stiff peaks form. Scoop whites on top of cottage cheese mixture. With a rubber spatula or wire whisk, gently fold whites in. Do not overmix or whites will deflate. Pour batter into prepared pan. Bake until center shows firmness when lightly touched, about 75 minutes. Turn off oven, leave door closed, and allow cheesecake to stand for 30 minutes.

Remove from oven and allow to cool completely. Chill before serving.

Frozen Cherry Pops

6 SERVINGS

1 tablespoon unflavored gelatin
1 cup white grape juice
1 pound soft tofu
1 cup pitted fresh or frozen
   sweet cherries
2 tablespoons safflower oil
⅓ cup honey

1 tablespoon unsweetened
   frozen orange juice
   concentrate
1 tablespoon lime juice
⅛ teaspoon almond extract
1 teaspoon vanilla extract

In a small saucepan, dissolve gelatin in grape juice. Heat to a boil, then reduce heat and continue to cook, stirring constantly, for 1 minute. Set saucepan in refrigerator.

Meanwhile, combine remaining ingredients in a food processor and whip until mixture is completely smooth and no flecks of tofu are visible. While processor is running, add gelatin mixture. Freeze in ice cube trays, or popsicle molds, or an 8 × 8-inch glass dish overnight.

Frozen Fruit Yogurt

4 SERVINGS

1 cup plain low-fat yogurt
1 cup fresh fruit (raspberries,
   blueberries, peaches,
   apricots, cherries, or kiwi
   fruit)

1 tablespoon honey
1 teaspoon vanilla extract

Freeze yogurt for 3 to 4 hours.

In a food processor or blender, puree the fruit, honey, and vanilla. Add frozen yogurt and combine. Refreeze for another 3 to 4 hours.

Just before serving, process again to smooth and serve immediately.

> VARIATION: To make a yogurt pie, scoop Frozen Fruit Yogurt into a baked 9-inch pie shell. Freeze. When ready to serve, cut into pieces with a knife that's been dipped into hot water.

Grape and Apple Cheesecake

10 SERVINGS

Cake
- 3 tablespoons toasted ground almonds
- 1½ pounds creamed cottage cheese
- ½ cup honey, warmed
- 3 eggs, room temperature
- 1 tablespoon butter, melted
- 1½ tablespoons orange juice
- 1 teaspoon grated orange peel
- ½ teaspoon vanilla extract
- ½ teaspoon almond extract
- 1 cup half-and-half
- 3 tablespoons sifted unbleached white flour
- ¼ teaspoon ground nutmeg
- 1 cup halved purple and green seedless grapes
- 1 green apple, unpeeled and thinly sliced

Glaze
- 1 tablespoon honey
- 1 tablespoon white grape juice
- 1 teaspoon butter

To prepare the cake: Preheat oven to 300°F. Butter a 9-inch springform pan.

Sprinkle bottom of pan with almonds, shaking pan to distribute evenly. Chill.

Press cottage cheese through a sieve into a large bowl. With an electric mixer, beat until smooth. Gradually beat in honey. Add eggs, 1 at a time, beating after each addition. Add butter, orange juice and peel, extracts, half-and-half, flour, and nutmeg. Beat until smooth. Pour into pan. Set pan on a jelly roll pan and bake for 1¼ to 1½ hours, or until set. Cool in oven with door slightly open for 1 hour. Transfer to a rack, remove sides of pan, and cool completely. Chill 3 hours or overnight.

Arrange grapes and apple slices on top of cake.

To prepare the glaze: In a small saucepan, combine honey, grape juice, and butter. Bring to a boil. Remove from heat and cool slightly. Brush top of cheesecake and fruit with glaze.

German Plum Tart

8 SERVINGS

2 pounds fresh Italian plums, halved and pitted	⅓ cup honey
¼ cup almonds	3 tablespoons water
1¼ cups whole wheat pastry flour, divided	2 eggs
1 teaspoon baking powder	1½ teaspoons vanilla extract
¼ teaspoon baking soda	⅛ teaspoon almond extract
4 tablespoons butter or margarine, softened	grated peel of ⅓ lemon

Preheat oven to 350°F.

Make a ½-inch cut into one end of each plum half. Set aside.

In a food processor, grind almonds with ½ cup of the flour until there are no visible traces of almonds, about 1 to 2 minutes. Add remaining flour, baking powder, and baking soda. Process with on-off turns until mixed. Transfer to a bowl or sheet of waxed paper and set aside.

Place butter or margarine in processor and process until a creamy, slightly foamy consistency. Add honey, water, eggs, extracts, and lemon peel. Process for 10 seconds to whip air into mixture. Add flour mixture. Process with 2 or 3 on-off turns just until flour is moistened.

Coat a 9-inch springform pan with vegetable cooking spray. Spread dough mixture evenly over bottom. Arrange plums in concentric circles over dough (place with pitted side up and tilt each piece at a 45-degree angle to the dough, with incision facing rim of pan). Cover almost the entire surface of dough, leaving only a very small space in center to allow you to test tart for doneness. Bake until a food pick inserted into center comes out clean, 35 to 50 minutes. Serve warm or at room temperature.

Jeweled Fruit Tart

6 SERVINGS

Pretty as a picture, this tart will dazzle all who see it. Use your imagination and seasonal fruits to compose gorgeous designs. Because the dough is soft and fragile, be sure to chill it as indicated for easier handling. Look for agar flakes in health foods stores.

Crust
- 1 cup whole wheat pastry flour
- 4 tablespoons butter or margarine, frozen
- 2 tablespoons honey
- 1 teaspoon vanilla extract
- 3 drops lemon extract
  grated peel of ⅓ lemon
- 2 to 4 tablespoons ice water

Glaze
- 1 teaspoon cornstarch
- 1½ teaspoons agar flakes
- ½ cup apple juice
- 1 tablespoon lemon juice
- 1½ teaspoons honey

Topping
- 1 pint strawberries
- 1 kiwi fruit

To prepare the crust: Place flour in a food processor. Cut butter or margarine into 1-inch pieces and add to flour. Using on-off turns, process until mixture resembles rolled oats. Add honey, extracts, and lemon peel. With machine running, pour just enough ice water through feed tube to make dough bunch up on blade, ready to form a ball. Stop machine instantly.

Lightly flour dough, place in a plastic bag, and refrigerate for 30 minutes. Flour dough again, flatten it with the heel of your hand, then place it between 2 sheets of waxed paper. Roll dough into a 12-inch circle. Peel off top layer of paper. Coat a 9-inch tart pan with a removable bottom with vegetable cooking spray.

Invert dough over tart pan. Peel off remaining paper. Gently press dough into pan, being careful not to stretch it. Trim excess off top and crimp edges, if desired. Prick dough all over with a fork and refrigerate for 30 minutes.

Preheat oven to 400°F.

Bake crust until lightly browned, 15 to 18 minutes. Allow to cool thoroughly before filling.

To prepare the glaze: Just before serving time, mix together cornstarch and agar in a small saucepan.

In a measuring cup, mix apple juice, lemon juice, and

honey. Stir into saucepan, and set aside for 5 minutes for agar to soften. Bring mixture to a boil, stirring constantly. When mixture is almost clear and agar has dissolved, remove from heat and allow to cool until mixture starts to gel, 7 to 10 minutes.

To prepare the topping: Hull strawberries, and cut berries into halves lengthwise. Peel kiwi and cut into thin slices. Arrange fruit decoratively on crust.

Spoon glaze over fruit, starting in center of tart. Glaze should set almost immediately upon contact with fruit. Serve immediately.

Poached Ginger Peaches

4 SERVINGS

4 peaches, halved	1 slice (1 × ¼-inch) ginger root
½ cup water	1 2-inch piece cinnamon stick
2 tablespoons lemon juice	dash of ground cinnamon

Preheat oven to 350°F.

Place peaches, round side up, in a baking dish. Combine water, lemon juice, ginger, and cinnamon stick and pour over peaches. Cover and bake for 30 minutes.

Remove ginger slice and cinnamon stick. Sprinkle with ground cinnamon and serve.

Honeydew Molds with Raspberry Sauce

4 SERVINGS

Molds
2 cups cubed honeydew melon, chilled
2 tablespoons lime juice
1 teaspoon honey
1 tablespoon unflavored gelatin
2 tablespoons cold water
2 tablespoons boiling water
4 mint sprigs for decoration

Sauce
10 ounces fresh or frozen raspberries (thawed if frozen)
½ teaspoon lime juice
1 tablespoon honey, or to taste

To prepare the molds: In a food processor or blender, puree honeydew, lime juice, and honey until smooth. Force mixture through a sieve into a medium-size bowl.

In a small bowl, sprinkle gelatin over cold water. Let stand 5 minutes to soften. Stir in boiling water and continue stirring to dissolve gelatin completely. Stir into honeydew mixture and mix well.

Rinse 4 4-ounce molds with cold water. Pour in honeydew mixture, cover, and freeze until completely frozen, at least 2 hours.

To prepare the sauce: Puree raspberries in a food processor or blender. Put through a sieve to remove seeds. Stir in lime juice and honey and chill.

To serve, spoon some sauce onto a serving dish. Place molds in very warm water for 15 to 20 seconds. Remove and run a sharp knife around the edge. Turn molds upside down so they drop onto plates and into sauce. Let stand about 20 minutes to thaw slightly. Decorate with mint sprigs.

Orange Angel Cake

10 SERVINGS

5 egg whites, at room
   temperature
¼ teaspoon cream of tartar
½ teaspoon orange extract
3 tablespoons honey

½ cup whole wheat pastry flour,
   sifted, divided
½ cup Orange Creme (recipe
   below)

Preheat oven to 325°F.

In a large bowl, beat egg whites at high speed until frothy. Add cream of tartar and beat until egg whites are stiff but not dry. Add orange extract and mix. Gradually add honey and mix thoroughly. Sprinkle 1 tablespoon of the flour over mixture, folding in carefully with a spatula until blended. Repeat until all the flour is used.

Spoon batter into a 9 × 5-inch loaf pan coated with vegetable cooking spray. Bake until lightly browned on top, about 35 minutes. Invert on cake rack and let cool completely.

Loosen cake with a knife. Remove from pan and slice lengthwise into 2 layers. Spread ¼ cup Orange Creme on bottom layer. Replace top layer and drizzle remaining ¼ cup Orange Creme over top.

Orange Creme

½ CUP

1 cup plain low-fat yogurt
1 teaspoon orange extract
1 teaspoon freshly grated orange
   peel

1 to 2 teaspoons honey

Spoon yogurt into a strainer lined with cheesecloth and place over a bowl to catch liquid. Let yogurt stand for 2 hours, then discard liquid.

In a small bowl, combine yogurt with orange extract, orange peel, and honey.

Orange Sorbet with Creamy Cashew Sauce

4 SERVINGS

Sorbet
2 cups orange juice
1 teaspoon finely grated orange peel
1 tablespoon lemon juice
⅓ cup honey
orange sections for decoration

Sauce
1 cup raw cashews
⅔ cup warm lemon tea or water
1 small banana
1 teaspoon lemon juice
½ teaspoon honey
dash of ground nutmeg

To prepare the sorbet: Combine orange juice, orange peel, lemon juice, and honey in a medium-size bowl, stirring to dissolve honey. Pour into an 8 × 8-inch dish. Freeze until solid, stirring occasionally to break up ice chunks. (You can process mixture in an ice cream maker according to manufacturer's directions.)

To prepare the sauce: Grind cashews in a blender until fine. Add tea and process until thoroughly combined. Strain through a fine sieve. Return to blender and add banana, lemon juice, honey, and nutmeg. Process until smooth and creamy.

To serve, spoon some sauce onto 1 side of each of 4 serving plates and top with a scoop of sorbet. Place 3 or 4 orange sections in a semicircle on the other side of the plate and serve immediately.

Raspberry Whip

4 SERVINGS

⅔ cup skim milk
¾ cup fresh raspberries

1 tablespoon honey
1 egg white

Place milk in freezer for 2 hours, or until it just begins to freeze.

Reserving 4 raspberries for garnish, puree remaining raspberries with honey in food processor.

Whip milk for about 7 minutes until thick.

Beat egg white until stiff but not dry. Fold egg white into whipped milk. Stir in raspberry puree and serve immediately, topping each serving with a reserved raspberry.

Strawberry Granita

4 SERVINGS

2 cups fresh or frozen strawberries
1 teaspoon ground ginger
1 cup tea

juice of 2 lemons, strained
3 tablespoons mild flavored honey
4 mint sprigs for decoration

In a food processor or blender, puree strawberries and ginger. Add tea, lemon juice, and honey and process until smooth. Pour into individual molds and freeze until solid, about 3 hours. Unmold onto individual shallow dishes, decorate with mint sprigs, and serve immediately.

Pear and Ricotta Pie

1 9-INCH PIE

Crust

1 cup whole wheat pastry flour
½ cup unbleached white flour
½ cup butter, cut into ½-inch
   pieces
2 to 4 tablespoons ice water

1 cup peeled, thinly sliced pears

Filling

2 cups part-skim ricotta cheese
4 eggs
¼ cup honey
1 teaspoon grated orange peel
1 teaspoon grated lemon peel
2 teaspoons orange juice
2 teaspoons lemon juice
1½ teaspoons unbleached white
   flour
¼ teaspoon ground cinnamon
⅛ teaspoon ground nutmeg
1¼ teaspoons vanilla extract
¼ teaspoon almond extract

Topping

2 large pears, peeled and thinly
   sliced
1 tablespoon lemon juice
2 cups apple juice
3 tablespoons orange
   marmalade

To prepare the crust: Stir whole wheat pastry flour and
unbleached white flour together in a medium-size bowl. Cut
butter into flours with a pastry blender, or two knives. Slowly
add ice water, a tablespoon at a time, until you can gather
dough into a ball. Flatten dough slightly and wrap with plastic
wrap. Refrigerate 1 hour. On a lightly floured surface or floured
waxed paper, roll out dough to form a 12-inch circle, ⅛ to
¼ inch thick. Fit into a 9-inch pie plate. Trim excess dough from
edges. Flute edges or press with a fork. Arrange the 1 cup of
pears in pie shell.

To prepare the filling: In a medium-size bowl, beat ricotta
until smooth and creamy. Add eggs and beat well. Beat in
honey gradually. Add orange and lemon peels, juices, flour,

cinnamon, nutmeg, and vanilla and almond extracts, beating until well-combined. Pour into pie shell. Bake in a preheated 350°F oven for 15 minutes. Reduce oven temperature to 325°F and bake another 45 minutes, or until filling is set. Cool on rack. Chill thoroughly.

To prepare the topping: Toss pears with lemon juice. In a medium-size skillet, bring apple juice to a boil. Add pears and cook for 1 minute, stirring constantly. Remove with a slotted spoon and drain well on paper towels. Arrange pears in a circle around the edge of the crust, overlapping the slices slightly. In a small saucepan, melt marmalade over low heat. Brush pears with marmalade. Chill.

Nutty Walnut Drops

3 DOZEN COOKIES

⅓ cup butter
⅓ cup maple syrup
½ teaspoon vanilla extract
¼ teaspoon finely grated lemon
    peel
1 cup whole wheat flour

2 tablespoons toasted wheat
    germ
2 cups chopped walnuts
1 tablespoon buttermilk
½ teaspoon baking soda

Preheat oven to 325°F. Lightly oil 2 baking sheets.

Warm butter and maple syrup in a small saucepan over low heat just until butter melts. Remove from heat and stir in vanilla and lemon peel.

In a medium-size bowl, mix together flour, wheat germ, and walnuts.

Put buttermilk into a cup. Stir in baking soda until dissolved. Add to dry ingredients along with butter mixture and stir just until combined. Drop the batter by the teaspoonfuls onto baking sheets and bake for 12 to 15 minutes, or until light golden brown.

Cool on wire racks. Store in a tightly covered container.

Oatmeal Raisin Cookies

2 TO 2½ DOZEN COOKIES

½ cup butter
½ cup honey or maple syrup
1 egg, beaten
1 tablespoon buttermilk
1 teaspoon vanilla extract
1 cup whole wheat flour

¼ cup brown rice flour
½ teaspoon baking soda
¼ teaspoon baking powder
⅛ teaspoon ground coriander
1 cup rolled oats
½ cup raisins

Preheat oven to 350°F. Lightly oil 2 baking sheets.

Melt butter in a small saucepan over low heat. Stir in honey or maple syrup. Cool mixture slightly, then stir in egg, buttermilk, and vanilla.

In a medium-size bowl, mix together whole wheat flour, brown rice flour, baking soda, baking powder, coriander, rolled oats, and raisins.

Stir the wet ingredients into the dry ingredients just until combined. Drop batter by the teaspoonfuls onto baking sheets, leaving enough room for cookies to spread, and bake for about 12 minutes, or until golden brown.

Index

A

Acorn squash, 39
Angel cake, orange, 189
Apple(s)
  caraway bread, 162
  cider vinegar dressing, 107
  and grape cheesecake,
    184
  grilled, on barley pilaf, 9
  and lemon sauce, 123
  and oat breakfast, 7
  rice salad, 51
  tart, 177
  terrine, 178
Apricot cream, 7
Apricot mousse, frozen, 178
Apricot-stuffed Cornish game
  hens, 95
Arugula, 48

B

Baliñas, 32
Banana splits, with apricot
  cream, 7
Barbecues, 133, 136-55
Barbecue sauce, 153
Barley and chicken soup, 98
Barley flour, 157
Barley pilaf, with grilled
  apples, 9

Bean and pear salad, 52
Beans, 48
  yard-long, in oyster sauce,
    29
Beef, stir-fry sandwiches, 124
Beet salad, 129
Belgian endive, 136
Beverages, breakfast, 5-6
Biscuits. See also Muffins
  buttermilk, 33
  and chicken, 92-93
  currant buttermilk, 164
Blender breakfasts, 1-6
Bok choy, 49
Boysenberries, 49
Braising, 23
Bread pudding, raspberry, 14
Bread(s), 131, 157-73
  apple caraway, 162
  chili con queso corn, 163
  cinnamon, currant, and
    walnut, 167
  dilled carrot, 159
  onion dill, 165
  orange spice, 166
  Parmesan, 160
  salt-free, 158
  seven-grain, 161
Breakfast(s), 1-19
  fast-fix blender, 1-2, 3,
    5-6
  importance of, 1

Broccoli and orange salad,
53
Broccoli and potato frittata,
8
Broccoli and seafood terrine,
86
Broiling, 23
fish, 71
Brown rice flour, 157
Brown sugar, 176
Butter, 131
prune, 14
unsalted, 175
Buttermilk, 24
Buttermilk biscuits, 33
currant, 164

C

Cake. See also Cheesecake
carrot, 180-81
orange angel, 189
Calorie-saving cooking, 22-23
Cappuccino, 5
Carrot(s)
bread, dilled, 159
cake, 180-81
muffins, 169
orange-glazed, 129
terrine, 54
Cashew and ginger sauce, 139
Cashew sauce, 190
Cheese. See also specific types
with chicken breasts, 94
and crackers, 24
low-fat, 23
mushroom sandwiches,
112
mushroom sauce, 113
with pasta and peas, 59

pesto pitas, 55
and rice pie, 111
and sprouts, 63
Cheesecake
crustless German, 181
grape and apple, 184
Cherry popsicles, 182
Chevre
with bean and pear salad,
62
with pasta and herb
sauce, 60
Chicken
and barley soup, 98
and biscuits, 92-93
breasts, with cheeses, 94
and fruit sandwiches, 111
grilled with mustards, 142
grilling tips for, 134
gumbo, 34
kabobs, 138
liver paté, 136
liver terrine, 137
low-calorie, 36, 41
peanut, 146
with pineapple, 36
poached, 31
sautéed with
strawberries, 99
spicy, with pork and
pineapple, 97
stock dressing, 107
terrine, 96
with winter vegetables, 125
yogurt patties, 109
Chili con queso corn bread,
163
Chili sauce
eggs with, 10
with shrimp, 30

Chinese white sauce, 106
Chutney, tomato, 11
Cinnamon caraway pancakes, 19
Citrus fruits, 48
Compote, prune, 15
Condiment, rhubarb and zucchini, 117
Cookies
    baking tips for, 176
    oatmeal raisin, 195
    walnut drop, 194
Cooking oils guide, iv-xvii
Corn bread, chili con queso, 163
Corn cakes, herb-pressed, 13
Cornish game hens
    apricot-stuffed, 95
    wild-rice, 91
Cornmeal, 157
Cornmeal muffins, 170
Corn pone pie, 10-11
Cottage cheese, 23
Crackers and cheese, 24
Cream cheese, 131
Cremes, orange, 189
Crepes, 2-4
    easy fillings and toppings for, 2
    fruit, 16
    whole wheat, 16
Crudites, low-calorie, 27
Cucumbers, in yogurt, 37
Cumin shrimp sauce, 119
Currant buttermilk biscuits, 164
Currant-walnut bread, 167
Curry
    potato, 63
    vinaigrette dressing, 149

D

Dairy products. *See also* Butter; Milk; Yogurt
    fresh, 175
    low-fat, 23-24
Desserts, 175-95. *See also* *specific types*
Dill sauce, with salmon, 84
Dip. *See also* Sauce
    dilled cucumber, 25
    horseradish, 26
    hummus, 26
    low-calorie, 24, 25-26
    red onion, 25
    rhubarb and zucchini, 117
Dressing(s), 47. *See also* Sauce
    curry vinaigrette, 149
    endive with walnut vinaigrette, 136
    herb, 118
    low-calorie, 24
    quick and easy, 107, 118
    vinaigrette, 52

E

Eggnog, carob, 5
Eggplant
    baked with garlic, 110
    with pasta in sesame sauce, 114
    salad, 140
    sesame, 65
    soup, 37
    spread, 145
Eggs
    with chili sauce, 10
    stuffed with Roquefort, 141
Endive, with walnut vinaigrette, 136

F

Fast-fix blender breakfasts,
1-2, 3, 5, 6
Fats, 21
Fillings, for crepes, 2-4
Fish, 70-88. *See also*
specific varieties
grilling tips for, 135
hors d'oeuvres, 32
soup, 76
varieties of, 72
Flounder, with tomato sauce,
77
Flour, 157
as thickener, 22
Fowl. *See* Poultry;
specific types
Frittata
baked onion, 51
broccoli and potato, 8
Fritters, baked oyster, with
tarragon sauce, 73
Fruit. *See also specific*
varieties
citrus, 48
crepes, 16
and curried chicken
sandwiches, 111
fresh, 176
juice blend, 6
kabobs, 8
salad, 57
tart, 186-87
and turkey salad, 121
unusual, 48-49
yogurt, frozen, 183

G

Ginger and cashew sauce, 139
Ginger peaches, 187

Gluten, 157
Gluten flour, 157
Goat cheese. *See* Chevre
Gooseberries, 49
Grains, 48, 157
Granita, strawberry, 191
Grape and apple cheesecake,
184
Greens. *See also* Tangerines
and greens
in torte, 58
Grilled foods, 133
Grilling tips, 134-35
Ground millet flour, 157
Guaco tacos, 112
Guava, 49

H

Haddock, herbed Parmesan,
128
Herb dressing, 118
Herbs, 47
Herb sauce, with pasta and
chevre, 60
Hoi sin sauce, 105
Honey, 175-76
Honeydew molds, 188
Hors d'oeuvres
low-calorie, 30, 32, 35
shrimp, 30
tomato, 35
Horseradish sauce, 154
Hummus, 26

K

Kabobs
chicken, 138
fruit, 8
Greek garden, 142
salad, seafood, 149

L

Lemon and apple sauce, 123
Lentil salad, 143
London broil, 144
Low-calorie, recipes, 21-45

M

Mackerel
    braised, 74
    salad, 81
Maple-nut muffins, 171
Maple syrup, 176
Margarine, 131
    unsalted, 175
Marinades, 133
Marinated foods, 132, 133
Meat loaf, garden, 141
Meats. See also Beef; Meat
    loaf; Veal
    grilling tips for, 134-35
    low-calorie, 21
    marinated, 133
Microwave recipes, 125-29
Milk. See also Buttermilk
    low-fat, 2, 23
    nonfat dry, 175
Milkshake, peanut butter, 6
Molasses, 176
Mousse, frozen apricot, 178
Muffins. See also Biscuits
    carrot, 169
    cornmeal, 170
    maple-nut, 171
    oatmeal-yeast, 172
    orange, 168
    overnight, 173
    rice, 67
Mushroom cheese sandwiches,
    112

Mushroom cheese sauce, 113
Mushrooms, stuffed, 120
Mussels, herb-steamed with
    rice pilaf, 79
Mustard dressing, 107
Mustard topping, 32

N

Neufchâtel cheese, 23
No-meat dishes, 47-67
Nonfat dry milk, 175

O

Oatmeal raisin cookies, 195
Oatmeal-yeast muffins, 172
Onion dill bread, 165
Onion frittata, 51
Onion tart, 61
Orange
    angel cake, 189
    creme, 189
    juice and vinegar
        dressing, 107
    muffins, 168
    sorbet, 190
    spice bread, 166
Oyster sauce, 29, 105
Oyster stew, 82

P

Paella, vegetable, 43
Pancakes, 2-4
    cinnamon caraway, 19
    pasta, 12
Parmesan bread, 160
Parsnips, cidered, 126
Passion fruit, 49

Pasta
  with chevre and herb
    sauce, 60
  with eggplant, pine nuts,
    and sesame sauce, 114
  with peas and cheese, 59
  quick and easy, 101-2,
    114-16
  with salmon and dried
    tomatoes, 115
  and salmon salad, 117
  with shrimp and saffron
    sauce, 116
  with spicy peanut
    sauce, 60
Pastacake, 12
Pastry flour, 175
Paté
  chicken liver, 136
  sandwiches, 148
Patties, chicken yogurt, 109
Peaches, poached ginger, 187
Peach sauce, 119
Peanut butter shake, 6
Peanut chicken, 146
Peanut sauce, 60
Pear charlotte, 179
Pear and ricotta pie, 192-93
Peas, and pasta with cheese,
  59
Peppers. See also Red
  pepper sauce, herbed
    chili and corn stuffed,
      56
    roasted, 43
    stuffed, 66
Pesto sandwich spread, 155
Picnics, 131-32, 136-55
Pie. See also Tart
  cheese and rice, 111
  corn pone, 10-11

  pear and ricotta, 192-93
  spinach, 42
Pilaf
  barley, with grilled
    apples, 9
  rice, 79
Pineapple
  relish, 85
  with spicy chicken and
    pork, 97
Pita, cheese pesto, 55
Pizza, 62
  low-calorie, 28
  quick and easy, 101-2
  20-minute, 122
Plum sauce, 139
Plum tart, 185
Poaching, 22
  fish, 71
Popsicles, cherry, 182
Pork and chicken with
  pineapple, 97
Pork and noodles, low-
  calorie, 44
Potato(es)
  baked, 22
  baked, with mustard
    topping, 32
  and blueberry salad, 53
  curry, 63
  salad(s), 64, 132
  tomato salad, 120
  toppings, 22, 50
Poultry, 60-70, 89-99
  frozen, 70
  low-calorie, 21
Prune butter, 14
Prune compote, 15
Pudding, raspberry bread,
  14
Pureed vegetables, 22

Q

Quick breads, 158
Quick and easy recipes, 101-29
Quick-fix dressing, 107
Quick sauces, 108

R

Radicchio, 48
Raisin and sweet potato
  scones, 15
Raspberry
  blend, 6
  bread pudding, 14
  sauce, with honeydew
    molds, 188
  whip, 191
Ratatouille, 147
Red pepper sauce, herbed, 113
Red snapper Neapolitan, 83
Red wine vinegar, 107
Rhubarb and strawberry soup,
  39
Rhubarb and zucchini
  condiment, 117
Rice
  and cheese pie, 111
  and dilled shrimp salad,
    140
  pilaf, with herb-steamed
    mussels, 79
  timbales, 67
  vinegar dressing, 107
  waffles, with strawberry
    sauce, 18
Ricotta, 23
Ricotta and pear pie, 192-93
Roquefort-stuffed eggs, 141
Roulades, sole and salmon, 31

Rutabagas, cooked, 127
Rye flour, 157

S

Saffron sauce, 116
Salad bar sandwiches, 118
Salade nicoise, 148
Salad(s), 47
  apple rice, 51
  bean and pear, 52
  broccoli and orange, 53
  crushed eggplant, 140
  dilled shrimp and rice,
    140
  lentil, 143
  mackerel, 81
  potato, 132
  potato and blueberry, 53
  quick and easy, 117,
    120-21, 129
  roasted potato, 64
  salmon and pasta, 117
  scallop, with pineapple
    relish, 85
  seafood kabobs, 149
  selecting ingredients
    for, 106-7
  sesame cucumber, 28
  spicy beet, 129
  tomato potato, 120
  turkey and fruit, 121
  warm salmon, 88
  winter fruit, 57
Salmon
  with dill sauce, 84
  with pasta and dried
    tomatoes, 115
  and pasta salad, 117
  salad, warm, 88

sandwiches, 150
and sole roulades, 31
steaks, marinated, 144
Salt-free breads, 158
Sandwich(es)
curried chicken and
fruit, 111
Mediterranean club, 145
mushroom cheese, 112
paté, 148
for picnics, 131
salad bar, with herb
dressing, 118
salmon, 150
stir-fry beef, 124
Sauce. See also Dressing(s);
Topping(s)
apple and lemon, 123
barbecue, 153
cashew and ginger, 139
chili, with eggs, 10
chili, with shrimp, 30
Chinese white, 106
creamy cashew, 190
dill, 84
herb, 60
herbed red pepper, 113
hoi sin, 105
horseradish, 154
low-calorie, 29-30
mushroom cheese, 113
oyster, 29, 105
pasta, 101
peach, 119
plum, 139
quick and easy, 113-14,
116, 119, 123, 127
raspberry, 188
saffron, 116
sesame, 114

shrimp with cumin, 119
soy, 17
spice, 106
spicy peanut, 60
stir-fry, 105-6
strawberry, 18
sweet and sour, 106
Szechuan, 106
tahini, 138
tarragon, 73
tomato, 77, 127
unusual and quick, 108
Sautéing
meats and poultry, 21
vegetables, 22
Sauté pan, 104
Scallops, with horseradish
sauce, 154
Scallop salad, with pineapple
relish, 85
Scones, raisin and sweet
potato, 15
Seafood. See Fish;
specific varieties
Seafood and broccoli terrine,
86
Seafood kabobs salad, 149
Sesame cucumber salad, 28
Sesame sauce, 114
Seven-grain bread, 161
Shortening, 175. See also
Butter; Margarine;
Vegetable(s), oil
Shrimp
in chili sauce, 30
dilled, 75
herb-poached, 38
hors d'oeuvres, 30
with pasta in saffron
sauce, 116

Shrimp (*continued*)
    and rice salad, 140
    sauce, 119
Snacks, low-calorie, 24
Sole and salmon roulades, 31
Solid shortening, 175
Sorbet, orange, 190
Soup. *See also* Stew
    chicken and barley, 98
    chunky turkey, with winter
      vegetables, 89
    eggplant, with pasta, 37
    fish, 76
    iced rhubarb and
      strawberry, 39
    Italian, 40
    low-calorie, 39, 40
Soy flour, 157
Soy sauce, 17
Spaghetti squash, cooked, 126
Spanakorizo, 42
Spice sauce, 106
Spinach terrine, 151
Spit roasting, 23
Spreads, 131-32
    eggplant, 145
    pesto, 155
    yogurt and dill, 150
Sprouts and cheese, 63
Squash
    acorn, 39
    confetti spaghetti, 126
Steak, London broil, 144
Steaming
    fish, 71
    vegetables, 22
Stew. *See also* Soup
    chicken gumbo, 34
    oyster, 82
    ratatouille, 147
Stewing, 23

Stir-fry, 102-4
    beef sandwiches, 124
    easy steps to, 104
    mix and match chart,
      102-3
    sauce, 105-6
Strawberry(ies)
    granita, 191
    sauce, on rice waffles,
      18
    with sautéed chicken,
      99
Sugar, 175
Sweeteners, 175-76
Sweet potatoes, maple
    mashed, 128
Sweet and sour sauce, 106
Swiss chard, stuffed, 152
Swordfish, grilled, 143
Szechuan sauce, 106

T
Tacos, guaco, 112
Tahini sauce, 138
Tamarillo, 49
Tangerines and greens, 59
Tarragon sauce, 73
Tart. *See also* Pie
    apple, 177
    fruit, 186-87
    onion, 61
    plum, 185
Terrine
    apple, 178
    carrot, 54
    chicken, 96
    chicken liver, 137
    seafood and broccoli,
      86
    spinach, 151
Tofu, 23

Tomato
  chutney, 11
  hors d'oeuvres, 35
  juice and vinegar
    dressing, 107
  potato salad, 120
  salmon and pasta with,
    115
  sauce
    with flounder, 77
    quick and easy, 127
Topping(s). *See also*
  Dressing(s); Sauce
  creamy mustard, 32
  low-calorie, 22
  for pancakes and waffles,
    2-4
  potato, 50
Torte, green vegetable, 58
Tortillas, 56-57
Triticale flour, 157
Trout
  fillet, 87
  herb-stuffed, 80
Tuna, poached in miso, 78
Turkey
  and fruit salad, 121
  Polynesian, 90
  soup with winter
    vegetables, 89

V

Veal, in apple and lemon
  sauce, 123
Vegetable(s), 47. *See also*
  specific varieties
  and chicken dish, 125
  crudites, 27
  favorites, 49
  ginger-pickled, 38

  Greek, 45
  kabobs, 142
  low-calorie, 22
  oil, 175
  paella, 43
  pickle, 45
  pureed, 22
  root, 48
  with turkey soup, 89
  unusual, 48-49
Vinaigrette dressings, 52
  endive with walnut, 136
Vinegar dressing, 107
Vinegar sautés, 21

W

Waffles, 2-4
  rice, with strawberry
    sauce, 18
Walnut drop cookies, 194
Wheat flour, 157
Whip, raspberry, 191
White wine vinegar dressing,
  107
Whole wheat crepes, 16
Whole wheat pastry flour, 175
Woks, 104
Wontons, 17

Y

Yeast breads, 158
Yogurt
  blends, 2
  and cucumber raita, 37
  and dill spread, 150
  dressing, 107
  frozen fruit, 183
  low-fat, 24